Practical Navigation for the Modern Boat Owner

Practical Navigation for the Modern Boat Owner

PAT MANLEY

WILEY NAUTICAL

John Wiley & Sons, Ltd

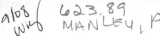
Copyright © 2008   John Wiley & Sons Ltd, The Atrium, Southern Gate, Chichester,
West Sussex PO19 8SQ, England
Telephone   (+44) 1243 779777

Email (for orders and customer service enquiries): cs-books@wiley.co.uk
Visit our Home Page on www.wiley.com

Other Wiley Editorial Offices

John Wiley & Sons Inc., 111 River Street, Hoboken, NJ 07030, USA

Jossey-Bass, 989 Market Street, San Francisco, CA 94103-1741, USA

Wiley-VCH Verlag GmbH, Boschstr. 12, D-69469 Weinheim, Germany

John Wiley & Sons Australia Ltd, 42 McDougall Street, Milton, Queensland 4064, Australia

John Wiley & Sons (Asia) Pte Ltd, 2 Clementi Loop #02-01, Jin Xing Distripark, Singapore 129809

John Wily & Sons Canada Ltd, 6045 Freemont Blvd. Mississauga, Ontario, L5R 4J3 Canada

Wiley also publishes its books in a variety of electronic formats. Some content that appears in print may
not be available in electronic books.

Library of Congress Cataloging-in-Publication Data

Manley, Pat.
   Practical navigation for the modern boat owner / Pat Manley.
      p. cm.
   Includes index.
   ISBN 978-0-470-51613-3 (cloth : alk. paper)
   1. Navigation–Handbooks, manuals, etc. 2. Global Positioning
System–Handbooks, manuals, etc. I. Title.
   VK555.M267 2008
   623.89–dc22

2008003730

British Library Cataloguing in Publication Data

A catalogue record for this book is available from the British Library

ISBN-13: 978-0-470-51613-3 (HB)

Typeset in 10/12 Futura by Thomson Digital, Noida, India
Printed and bound in Italy by Printer Trento, Trento

Contents

Cover points

- If you wonder why your in-car navigator shows that you are in a field – Read on
- If you wonder why your in-car navigator takes you on farm tracks – Read on
- If you think that the electronic charts on your chartplotter are accurate – Read on
- If you want to know the depth of water over the rocks – Read on
- If you think pressing 'GO TO' will take you safely to your destination – Read on

Foreword

The methods of navigation used by the modern boat owner have changed quite rapidly from the traditional methods still currently taught. This doesn't make the old methods wrong; it just means that the emphasis has changed.

With GPS used in many cars, the level of computer skills of the general public being high, and the so-called paperless office, the modern boat owner desires a different approach to navigation.

'Practical Navigation for the Modern Boat Owner' will lead you through all aspects of navigation of your boat in a logical order. The pencil and paper chart part of the subject is not introduced until it's demonstrated that some knowledge of traditional navigation is necessary. This practical approach to the subject will ensure that although the modern electronic methods of navigation remain at the forefront, the reader will never be lacking in sufficient knowledge to navigate his/her boat safely in any circumstance.

Proper passage planning is not only desirable, but it is also a legal requirement. This topic is thoroughly covered in an entirely practical manner.

The boat owner cannot rely entirely on electronic navigation for pilotage. Pilotage will introduce the well-established and practical aspects of entering and leaving a harbour or anchorage.

Radar is another area where legally the boat owner is required to know how to use this valuable tool. Again, this topic is approached using a practical and easily understood approach.

Introduction

When I gained my Flight Navigator's License in 1973, other than when I was actually on the ground, I never knew where I was, only where I had been! By the time you had worked out and plotted a fix, you were at least 60 miles further on. Even when I flew Boeing 747s, without a Flight Navigator, the inertial navigation system, which used three onboard gyroscopic platforms to measure acceleration in all three planes to determine where you were, could be 10 miles in error by the time you had flown 12 hours. Incidentally, the Apollo spacecraft to the moon used only one of these inertial systems for navigation!

Modern airliners use a combination of inertial navigation systems continually updated by automatically tuning into ground-based aids to remove any inherent errors. This has the huge benefit of using at least three different types of data on three completely separate systems to continuously monitor each other for errors, which if found are reported to the pilots.

The first time that I ever knew where I was all the time was when I started using GPS on board my own yacht, assuming of course that what it was telling me was correct.

Fortunately for me, I had around 10 million miles of 'real' navigation behind me and I knew when I could trust my GPS and when to treat it with a certain amount of suspicion.

My aim in this book is to show you how to use all the navigation tools at your disposal to the best advantage and to be able to weigh up which ones to place more reliance on according to the circumstances.

To me, navigation has always been more than a means to an end, and I hope you will get as much enjoyment out of it as I do.

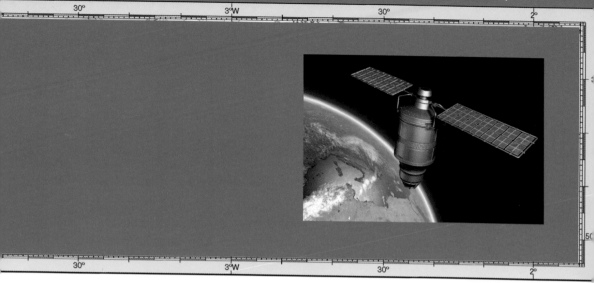

The Global Positioning System

How Your GPS Receiver Tells You Which Satellites It Can See
How GPS Works
Accuracy of the Fix
GPS Blackout
Deliberate Interference
GPS Is Line of Sight
Selective Availability
Differential GPS
Wide Area Augmentation Service
Switch-On Delays
Measurement of Speed
Measurement of Course
Measurement of Heading
Errors in COG and SOG

The original global positioning system (GPS) consists of 24 satellites orbiting the Earth at a distance of around 11 000 miles. Each orbits once every 12 hours in six orbital plains, so there will be between five and eight satellites in view at any time, from any point on the Earth's surface. The drawing here shows only three orbital plains for clarity.

Simplified GPS satellite constellation

There are a number of spare satellites in orbit in case of failure and each satellite has a life expectancy of about 7 years. New satellites are launched by the US military as required.

Fears about the American monopoly of accurate position fixing amongst non-USA countries have lead to the establishment of GLONASS (a Russian system) and the pending establishment of GALLILEO (a European system). They work in a similar manner and new versions of GPS receiver may be able to operate with any system.

How Your GPS Receiver Tells You Which Satellites It Can See

On startup, a GPS receiver starts looking for satellites and will display a page showing you its sky view all around the horizon. The outer ring is the horizon, the inner ring is at an elevation of 45 degrees and the centre represents the position in the sky vertically overhead (the zenith). The predicted positions of satellites are shown as empty circles which become coloured when a satisfactory satellite signal is received. The serial number of the satellite is shown in the circle. Alongside the diagrams are vertical bars representing the signal strength (in fact the signal-to-noise ratio or quality of the signal) and again each bar is numbered. In this way, you can see the number of satellites and the quality of the signals being received in order to form an idea of how good a fix you are likely to get. There's often a number giving an indication of the fix accuracy, more of which later.

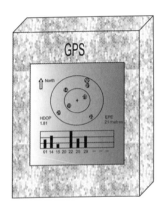

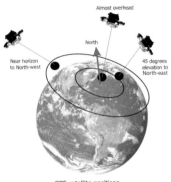

GPS satellite positions

How GPS Works

Timing

In order to find its position on the Earth's surface, a GPS receiver needs to find its distances from at least four satellites. Theoretically, it needs only three, but the clock on the receiver is not accurate enough to allow this.

Distance is measured by measuring the time taken for the GPS signal to travel from the satellite to the receiver. As the time taken is only 0.06 second for a

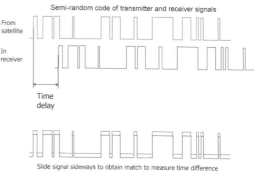

Semi-random code of transmitter and receiver signals

From satellite

In receiver

Time delay

Slide signal sideways to obtain match to measure time difference

Measuring the time taken for the GPS signal to reach the GPS receiver

satellite immediately overhead, an error of one thousandth of a second would give an error of 200 miles! Each satellite has an onboard 'Atomic Clock', which is super accurate, but for each receiver to be similarly equipped, GPS would not be a practical proposition.

Satellites transmit a semi-random signal, which the receiver matches with its own semi-random signal. The distance the receiver has to move its own signal to get a match is a measure of the time difference and a range can then be calculated. It's a bit like matching continually repeated barcodes in reality. This is accurate enough to get a first guess at the distance.

Fixing Position with GPS

If the distance to the satellite is calculated by the receiver, it can be plotted as a *position line*, where any place on the Earth's surface is the same distance from the satellite. The receiver must lie somewhere on that position line.

If the distances from two more satellites are calculated and plotted, the receiver must lie on all three lines. Normally, this can occur at only one point on the Earth's surface and so that must indicate the position of the receiver.

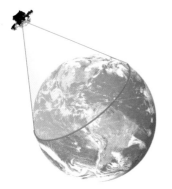

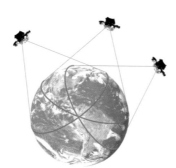

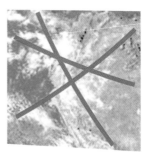

Cocked hat

Because of small inaccuracies in the receiver's clock, there will be an error in its position. The position lines will not intersect at the same point and will form what is known as a *cocked hat*.

Pseudo Range

A clever trick within the receiver converts the ranges into *pseudo* ranges, which allows them to be shuffled around within certain limits.

The range from a fourth or even more satellites is calculated and added to the *fix*.

The extra position line(s) allows the timing error to be determined and this results in a good fix, where all the position lines intersect at only one point.

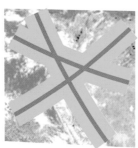

Pseudo range

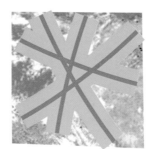

Fourth satellite

Good fix

Accuracy of the Fix

With range being calculated using the time taken for the signal to travel between the satellite and the receiver, any variation in the speed of the signal and the actual path followed will lead to errors.

Errors due to these effects will normally amount to no more than ±15 metres for 95% of the time, being made up from the following:

Range rings at 25 metres spacing

Normal GPS errors

- ionospheric effects, ±10 metres;
- ephemeris errors, ±2.5 metres;
- satellite clock errors, ±2 metres;
- multipath distortion, ±1 metre;
- tropospheric effects, ±0.5 metre;
- numerical errors, ±1 metre or less.

With my boat moored in the marina, normal GPS errors were plotted as shown over an 8 hour period. Although most were contained within the 25 metre diameter circle, one was almost 100 metres in error. This is perfectly normal GPS performance.

GPS Blackout

Solar flares can cause a complete GPS signal blackout on the sunlit side of the Earth's surface. In 2006 flares on the 5th and 6th of December caused profound and severe effects to GPS receivers causing a large number of them to stop tracking satellites. Professor Dale Gary of the New Jersey Institute of Technology said 'This solar radio burst occurred during a solar minimum, yet produced as much as 10 times more radio noise than the previous record ... at its peak, the burst produced 20000 times more radio emission than the entire rest of the Sun. This was enough to swamp GPS receivers over the entire sunlit side of the Earth'.

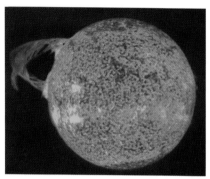

Solar flares can cause significant GPS errors even disablement of satellites

The Solar flare cycle covers a period of 11 years.

Deliberate Interference

The strength of the radio signals carrying the GPS data is very low and can easily be interfered with. Enemies can deliberately try to disrupt signals in a relatively small local area and military agencies regularly deliberately interfere with the signals to judge the results. These tests are promulgated in advance.

GPS Is Line of Sight

A GPS receiver must be able to 'see' a satellite in order to receive its signal. If buildings, cliffs or trees obstruct that line of site, the signal from that satellite will not be received and the accuracy of the fix may be degraded. It's possible that the signal may be

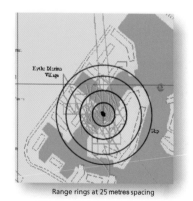

Range rings at 25 metres spacing

GPS errors with 'selective availability'

received as it bounces off another surface so it will take longer time to arrive and will give an inaccurate range. Again this can degrade the fix accuracy.

The signal can penetrate some solid surfaces, such as glass, GRP and canvas, and it is sometimes possible for a receiver antenna mounted inside the boat to work satisfactorily.

Selective Availability

Originally, civilian users had their signals deliberately degraded by the US military inducing a randomly varying error, known as *selective availability*, ensuring that accuracy was no better than 100 metres for 95% of the time. This selective availability has been switched off, but the US military may reintroduce it, without warning, at any time. This must always be considered a possibility. On the accompanying chart, the error that disappears northward off the chart was over 800 metres.

Errors that occur from a corrupt satellite signal will be incorporated into the fix by a GPS receiver and can lead to very large errors, measured in miles, and will continue until the satellite is switched off by the monitoring team, which could take up to one and a half hours.

Differential GPS

A GPS receiver fixed in one place will know exactly where it is. Any position derived from the received GPS signals can be compared with its known position and any error deduced. If this error was transmitted to the nearby GPS receivers, they could take account of this error in deducing their own position to give a much more accurate result, with a 95% probability error of 3 metres. This is known as *differential GPS* (DGPS).

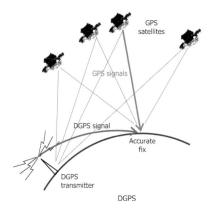

To take advantage of this, the GPS receiver needs both a separate DGPS receiver and to be within range of a DGPS station, usually about 200 miles. This is commonly used for survey GPS and was beginning to be common for leisure users until selective availability was switched off, when its need for normal leisure use disappeared because of the inherent 15-metre accuracy.

Wide Area Augmentation Service

Wide Area Augmentation Service (WAAS) uses a network of ground stations to monitor the GPS position accuracy. The error corrections are sent to two master stations, which in turn send error correction information to the constellation of satellites. The continuously varying error correction information is broadcast by the satellites and is then available to all WAAS compatible GPS receivers. The 95% error is then reduced to 7.5 metres. Manufacturers usually optimistically claim a 3-metre accuracy. Integrity monitoring is part of this system, so anomalous

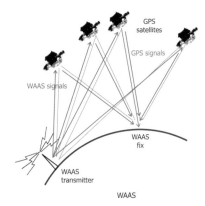

signals from under-performing satellites are automatically discarded.

WAAS is available only in the United States of America, but European Geostationary Navigation Overlay Service (EGNOS) and the Japanese Multi-Functional Satellite Augmentation System (MSAS) provide the same service in areas covered by these. A WAAS compatible receiver will operate with EGNOS and MSAS.

Range rings at 25 metres spacing

WAAS GPS errors

The Modern GPS Receiver

Modern GPS receivers normally have 12 or more channels which can receive data from 12 different satellites simultaneously. Satellites are moving fairly rapidly along their paths and the ability of the receiver to 'lock' onto a large number of satellites means that they are always using the best data available. It also means that their 'startup' times are very quick.

The oldest receivers have very few channels, so they have to divide their time between using data from only one or a few satellites and searching for new ones. They are inherently slow.

A modern GPS receiver

Switch-On Delays

Cold Start

When a new GPS receiver is first switched on, it has no idea of the time, date, where it is or where the satellites are. As the information about the whereabouts of the satellites is transmitted only every 12.5 minutes, it will be some time before the GPS can compute its first fix. This is known as a *cold start*.

Hot Start

When the GPS is switched in the same geographical position as when it was switched off, it knows where to expect the satellites to be, the date and the time, so modern 12 channel receivers can compute their first fix very quickly.

Warm Start

If the GPS receiver has been moved since it was last switched off, it will take longer time than a hot start but much less than a cold start.

Measurement of Speed

There is nothing inherent in the GPS signals that measure speed. However, the receiver does have a lot of built-in information that it can use to present useful information. Once the GPS receiver has worked out its position, it can use its knowledge of the shape and size of the Earth to determine the distance between any two points, so that once it is in motion it can work out the distance between two fixes, and taking the time taken to travel this distance it can deduce its speed. This speed is the *speed over the ground* (SOG), not to be confused with the speed through the water.

Fix at 0904

Fix at 0903

Distance travelled in 1 minute = 0.2 nautical miles

Speed over ground (SOG) = 12 knots

SOG Is Not Boat Speed

Boat speed is the speed of the boat through the water and is displayed on the water speed display. Wind, waves and tide will cause the speed over the ground to differ from the water speed.

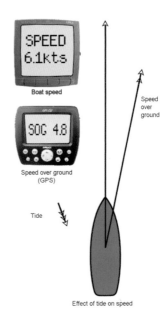

Boat speed

Speed over ground (GPS)

Tide

Speed over ground

Effect of tide on speed

Measurement of Course

The GPS signal contains no information on the direction in which the boat is moving. Because the GPS receiver knows the shape of the Earth, it can determine the direction that it has travelled from one fix to another. This *course over the ground* (COG) is exactly what it says and may not be the same as the course steered by the boat.

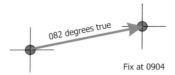

Fix at 0904

Fix at 0903

Because the GPS receiver knows the shape of the Earth, it can calculate the bearing of the second fix from the first. It is thus capable of calculating the course over the ground (COG)

COG Is Not Heading

The heading is the direction that the boat is pointing and is displayed on the compass. The wind, waves and tide can push the boat sideways over the ground, and it's this movement over the 'ground' that is displayed as COG. Only in calm conditions with no tide running will the heading and COG be the same.

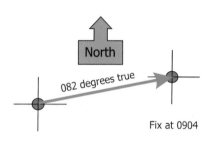

Tide

Heading being
steered 100

COG 113

Course over
ground 113

The effect of tide on heading

Measurement of Heading

GPS can't measure the boat's heading and can measure only the COG. Once the GPS receiver is moving, because it can determine COG, it knows the direction of true north. We will find, later in this book, that some instruments, such as radar and chartplotters, can make use of heading information to allow the display to be aligned with north to give a *north up* display. Although GPS can provide this information, there are two disadvantages: The information is available only once the boat is in motion and the alignment is based on COG rather than which way the boat is pointing.

North

082 degrees true

Fix at 0904

Fix at 0903

Once the GPS receiver is moving
it can determine the direction of North

Errors in COG and SOG

Any random errors in the fixes used to calculate COG and SOG will produce errors in speed and course displayed on the GPS.

The rate at which the GPS position is updated is very rapid, but to minimise the effect of random errors, COG and SOG are averaged over about 5 seconds, by default, although the user may alter this time. The longer the time interval, the steadier the reading, but the slower the response to a real alteration of heading or speed.

If the error between two fixes were 15 metres, one to port and the next to starboard, the error in COG over a 5-second period at 6-knots speed could be greater than 45 degrees. Similarly, with similar errors, but in the direction of movement, the SOG displayed could be in error by 6 knots! With selective availability switched off, the normal

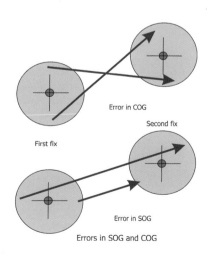

Error in COG

Second fix

First fix

Error in SOG

Errors in SOG and COG

situation, random errors are likely to be very small, and COG and SOG are generally stable and accurate. With the default setting for the 'averaging time', watch the COG and SOG at a constant speed and heading to get an idea of how they respond in normal conditions.

If selective availability is switched on by the US military, the accuracy of COG and SOG will deteriorate significantly.

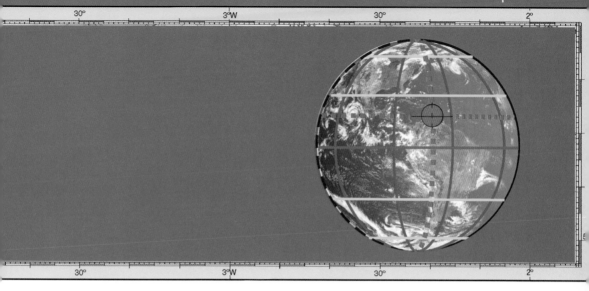

Our Address on the Earth's Surface

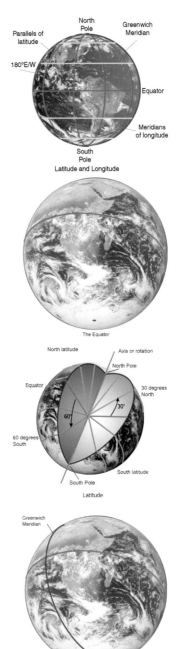

If you need to find someone, you need their address. To do this on planet Earth, an invisible, theoretical grid has been overlaid on the Earth's surface by geographers. This grid of *Latitude and Longitude* allows us to define any point on the Earth's surface with as much accuracy as we wish.

Latitude and Longitude

The Equator

The Earth spins on an axis through the North and the South Poles. Any circle running around the Earth's maximum circumference is known as a *great circle*. The Equator is a great circle at right angles to the spin axis and equidistant between the poles.

The Equator

Latitude

Latitude is defined as the angle in degrees between the Equator, the centre of the Earth and a point on the Earth's surface. If the point is between the Equator and the North Pole, it's called north latitude and if between the Equator and the South Pole, it's called south latitude. A circle can be drawn through all points of the same latitude, this circle being a *small circle* as its circumference is less than the Earth's, and it is parallel to the Equator. There are an infinite number of points on the Earth's surface with the same latitude, so latitude by itself cannot define our address.

Latitude

Greenwich Meridian

A half great circle joining the North and the South Poles and running through Greenwich Observatory in London, England is called the Greenwich Meridian. This forms the datum from which the other half of our address is obtained.

Greenwich Meridian

Longitude

The angle in degrees between the Greenwich Meridian where it crosses the Equator, the centre of the Earth and another point on the Equator is called the *longitude*. It is

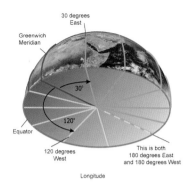

called west longitude if it's west of the Greenwich Meridian and east longitude if it's east of the Greenwich Meridian. All points on the Earth's surface having the same longitude lie on a great circle running through both poles and is known as a meridian of longitude.

Our Address

The combination of the latitude and the longitude of the point provides a unique address on the Earth's surface. We can now tell someone else where we are and also find the address of a place we may wish to visit.

Address is 22 degrees North, 66 degrees West
Our address on the Earth's surface

International Date Line

With the Earth spinning around its axis once per day, the date clicks up a day at a time at midnight. If you were to travel around the world faster than the Earth's rotation, you would have time travel, so a mechanism needs to be found to stop that happening and the answer is the International Date Line. When you cross the 180-degree meridian, the date changes, either jumping forward a day– if you're travelling west – or dropping back a day – if you're travelling east. For much of its length, the 180-degree meridian is the International Date Line as well. However, in order that the jump doesn't occur over land, the date line has some wiggles, both east and west, so that the whole of any country or territory is on the same date.

International date line
International date line

Measurement of Latitude and Longitude

One degree is divided into 60 minutes. Normally, 1 minute is divided into 60 seconds; however, this is rather cumbersome when measuring on a chart, so for navigation purposes, 1 minute is divided using the decimal notation; so, we write down (and say) degrees, minutes and tenths (or hundredths or thousandths) of a minute.

13

So, for instance, 35 degrees, 43 minutes and 456-thousandths of a minute is written as 35° 43.456'.

Thus, we write a position as

> Latitude 35 degrees 43.456 minutes North.
> Longitude 026 degrees 12.765 minutes East.

We use the format,

> Latitude dd° mm.mmm'.
> Longitude ddd° mm.mmm'.

The maximum number of degrees latitude is 90 and the maximum number of degrees longitude is 180.

Distance and Direction

In order to navigate anywhere, we need to determine both the distance and the direction to our destination.

Distance

Most of us are used to miles or kilometres, but these are not the measurements used at sea or in the air. The problem is that these measurements are not related to the geometry of the Earth and so the user has to have a scale of distance to use whenever the distance must be measured.

The Nautical Mile

The nautical mile is directly related to the circumference of the Earth. One degree (60 minutes) of latitude is equal to 60 nautical miles. Thus,

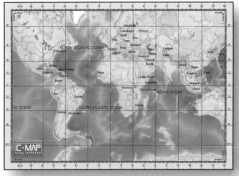

A chart drawn using a 'Mercator' projection

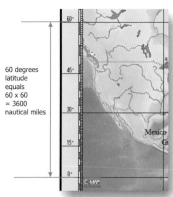

60 degrees
latitude
equals
60 x 60
= 3600
nautical miles

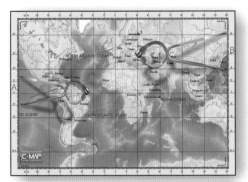

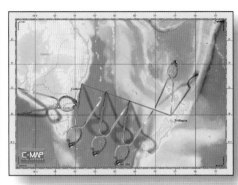

Use latitude scale at same latitude as distance to be measured

'Walking the dividers'

- One nautical mile equals one minute of latitude.

Distance can be measured directly from the latitude graticule of the chart. The distance from the Equator to 60 degrees North is $60 \times 60 = 3600$ nautical miles.

If you look carefully at a chart, you will see that the latitude graticule doesn't have constant spacing. This is especially true on a Mercator projection, where the distance between each 10 degrees of latitude gets progressively greater. Where a chart covers a large portion of the Earth's surface, this is especially critical when measuring distance.

So, when measuring distance, we should use the region of the latitude graticule at almost the same latitude as the distance to be measured. If the distance between two points is longer than the 'open' distance of the dividers, measure a convenient length on the latitude graticule and then 'walk' the dividers along the line, counting each step. Measure the remaining small distance and add this to the number of steps and you have the total distance.

Under no circumstances should you use the longitude graticule to measure distance. Only at the Equator it does give approximately the distance, and as you move further away the error increases. At 30 degrees North, 1 minute of longitude equals 0.866 nautical mile and at 60 degrees North (or South) it's only half a mile. At the poles, it is of course 0 nautical mile.

When you change chart scales, check the latitude graticule carefully to ensure that you know what each coloured part

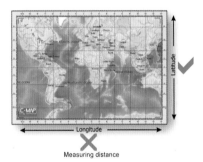

Measuring distance

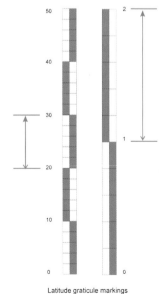

Latitude graticule markings

represents: 1 mile, 5 miles, 10 miles, etc. It is really easy to make a mistake, especially when one chart is lying on top of another and you can see both latitude graticules.

Direction

All meridians pass through the North Pole and so all meridians define the direction of *true* north. It is true because it refers to the geographical pole. For this reason, we measure direction relative to a meridian. On a Mercator chart, the meridians are parallel to each other, so direction can be measured relative to any meridian on the chart.

A conical projection implies that none of the meridians are parallel, and so direction must be measured relative to the meridian *nearest* to where you wish to measure the direction.

Never measure direction relative to the chart's border because this may not be aligned with true north.

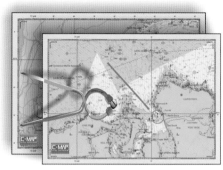
Wrong scale!

Line crosses each meridian at a different angle

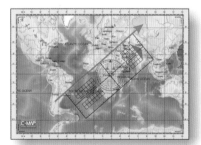
Measuring direction with a course plotter

Meridians not aligned with chart border

Magnetic North Pole

The true North Pole is on the Earth's spin axis. However, this is not where a magnetic compass points. The compass needle is attracted towards the *magnetic* North Pole, which at the present time is situated in the north of Canada, about 800 miles south of the true North Pole. It moves slowly, but noticeably and the annual value must be used for navigation.

Variation

The angular difference between the direction of true north and magnetic north is called *variation* and its value is indicated on a chart, together with its annual change. Variation may be east or west of true north and is annotated accordingly.

Deviation

Because of the influence of the boat and its equipment, the compass rarely points at the magnetic pole, this error being called *deviation*. Deviation is specific to your boat, changes according to the heading (and heel) of your boat, and must be reassessed annually as it will change with time and any additional equipment fitted. Compass correction is dealt with in a later chapter.

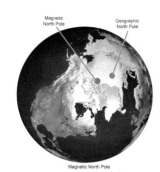

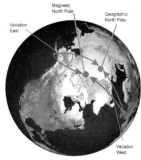

Measuring Direction on the Chart

There are a number of different instruments for measuring direction, and users have their favourites. Probably, the two easiest to use on a small chart table are the 'Portland' type course plotter and the parallel rule.

Course Plotter

This plotter needs nothing except a meridian to line up on, although in practice, parallels of longitude may be used as well on the type of chart normally used.

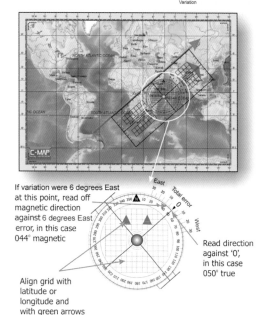

- Place the edge of the plotter on the line joining two places with the main arrow pointing in the direction of travel.

- Rotate the centre knob to align the grid on the central wheel with the latitude/longitude graticule.

- Read off the direction against the '0' on the centreline of the plotter.

- Variation can be applied as you work using the east or west error offset. This allows the direction to be read directly from the plotter.

If variation were 6 degrees East at this point, read off magnetic direction against 6 degrees East error, in this case 044° magnetic

Align grid with latitude or longitude and with green arrows pointing north

Read direction against '0', in this case 050° true

Measuring direction with a course plotter

Parallel Rule

To use a parallel rule easily, there needs to be a *compass rose* on the chart. A compass rose is a 'protractor', aligned with true north, printed on the chart. An 'inner' concentric protractor aligned with magnetic north may also be shown. The amount of variation and the year of its validity at that point are shown together with the annual change and its direction of change.

There are likely to be several compass roses on each chart. The variation at each rose may be different.

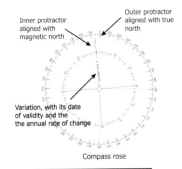

Inner protractor aligned with magnetic north

Outer protractor aligned with true north

Variation, with its date of validity and the the annual rate of change

Compass rose

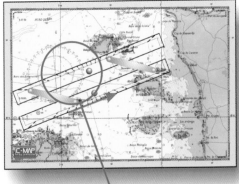

- Place the edge of the parallel rule along the direction to be measured.

- Open up the parallel rule until the other edge passes through the centre of the nearest compass rose.

- If it wouldn't reach far enough, 'walk' the rule across the chart until it reaches the centre of the compass rose, being careful that its direction isn't altered.

Magnetic or True Direction?

All paper charts give direction in degrees true. You can convert these directions to magnetic if you wish. All magnetic compasses show direction in degrees magnetic (with an error due to deviation if this is applicable).

When steering the boat using a magnetic compass to determine the direction, we need to know the 'course to steer' in degrees magnetic. It is, therefore, traditional to convert all directions to magnetic.

Align parallel rule with direction and open it up so that it passes through centre of compass rose, 'walking' it if necessary

Read off direction on compass rose, in this case 069 degrees true or 074 degrees magnetic

Measuring direction with a parallel rule

Global positioning system (GPS) and electronic chartplotters have the Earth's variation chart built in, so that if they know where they are, they will know the local variation. Therefore, if you wish, you can tell the GPS or chartplotter to show all directions as degrees magnetic. I prefer to do this as I can compare all direction information directly with my magnetic compass without having to tax my poor old brain.

If you have an electronic compass, and use your magnetic compass only as a back up, you can use true direction if you prefer. If you do so, ensure that all the 'electronics' use true direction and that your crew understands what you are doing. At the present time, this is a non-standard procedure, but in the future, this may become the norm.

The Flat Earth

Have you ever tried peeling an orange and laying the peel out on a flat surface? Difficult, isn't it?

As soon as you try and make a chart, paper or electronic, you run up against the problem of transforming a spherical surface into a flat sheet. It's fine if the area covered is no bigger than a football ground, but if you want a sizeable portion of land or sea, you just can't do it easily.

Strictly speaking, mariners and aviators use charts, while maps are used on land, though for serious navigation on land, such as in the desert, and then we are back to charts again.

Chart Projections

Ever since man realised that the Earth wasn't flat, many different ways of depicting the Earth's surface have been tried. All have disadvantages. From looking at some maps, many people think that Greenland is a massive island, bigger than South America, Australia or the United States of America. In reality, Greenland is smaller than Algeria and less than a quarter the size of the United States of America and one-third the size of Australia. So why is this confusion?

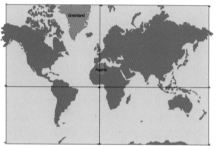

The shape's right, the size is wrong

There is no projection that shows *both* correct size *and* correct shape of the continents. If we have the correct shape, we have the wrong size and vice versa. So it depends what use is to be made of the chart or map, which of the many projections is chosen. It doesn't matter if we are considering a paper chart or an electronic one; they all suffer from the same problems. There are many projections that are used by cartographers, but as this is a practical book, we'll just look at a couple of basic principles. Should you wish to do any long distance sailing, you'll need to study this topic further.

Mercator projection

Mercator Projection

Let us imagine a translucent Earth with a powerful light source at its centre. If we were to wrap a cylinder of paper around the globe, the outline of the land would be projected onto the inner surface of the cylinder of paper. If we now trace the outline onto the paper and unfurl it, we would have a chart drawn using the Mercator projection.

19

We can immediately see that instead of the parallels of latitude being equally spaced, they get further apart as we go towards the poles. This is the projection that makes Greenland (2 172 000 square kilometres) look hugely bigger than the slightly larger Algeria (2 382 000 square kilometres). The meridians, which should meet at the poles, are parallel. Mercator charts are useful for some types of navigation, but we need to be aware of the changing scale of the chart as we move north or south of the Equator. The direction of north is always 'vertical', towards the top of the chart. It is impossible to show the polar regions.

Conical Projections

Again we need to imagine a translucent Earth with a light at the centre. This time, we wrap the paper in the shape of a cone which touches the Earth somewhere north (or south) of the Equator. The area that we're mapping influences where we make the tangent to the surface. We can see that the parallels of latitude are parallel, but curved and the meridians are straight, but converge towards the closest pole.

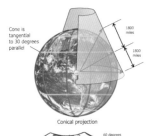

Within a reasonable distance of the tangential parallel, scale is much more consistent. Look at how Greenland and Algeria are much closer to their proper areas. The direction of north (or south) is not constant but towards some invisible 'vanishing' point. Again we cannot represent the polar regions.

Conical projection

Polar Projections

The only way to show the polar regions on a navigation chart is by having a flat sheet of paper sitting directly on the pole. All parallels of latitude are concentric circles about the pole and meridians are straight lines radiating from the pole. Scale is correct only at the pole. When situated at the pole, all directions are south from the North Pole or north from the South Pole.

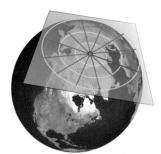

Polar projection

The Spherical Earth and 'Map Data'

In fact the Earth isn't a sphere, it's an oblate spheroid, flattened at the poles and with bumps on it. These bumps are not the mountains and oceans, but irregularities which depart from the regular shape of the Earth. They occur over areas large enough for the mapmakers to take them into account when producing maps of their country. Because the bumps effecting each country is slightly different, each national map making organisation has used complicated formulae which best represent their part of the world, so that other map makers know what is going on, each formula is designated a code, known as a *map datum*. This is printed on the chart. For example, in the United Kingdom, the map datum is referred to as OSGB36, which stands for Ordnance Survey of Great Britain, 1936, the year in which it was devised. In the United States of America, it's NAD27, but this is then split into versions for different areas and in Australia it's Aus Geo 66.

Having different map data mattered not one jot. Although the same latitude and longitude may have given positions several hundred metres from their proper position, the 'accuracy' of position fixing was such that these errors were undetectable. Not so now, where even amateur yachtsmen can fix their position to within 15 metres most of the time.

This difficulty was realised when GPS was being designed and a new international datum was produced which, although very complex, allowed for the true shape of the Earth everywhere. This datum is known as WGS84 – World Geodetic System 1984.

Paper Charts

Only very recently have paper charts been drawn using WGS84 as the datum. The majority of paper charts use their local datum, so if the GPS receiver is set to give position in WGS84 format, which it will by default, the position when plotted on the paper chart will be in error by as much as a couple of hundred metres (600 feet). This is of significance only if you are trying to use your GPS for 'close quarters' navigation, which you should never do in isolation in any case. Paper charts

> *Positions* are referred to Ordnance Survey of Great Britain (1936) datum.
>
> Satellite-derived positions
>
> Positions obtained from satellite navigation systems are normally referred to WGS 84 Datum; such positions should be moved 0.03 minute *southward* and 0.10 minute *eastward* to agree with this chart.

Map datum

printed subsequently to the introduction of GPS should be annotated with the datum used and any correction to be applied. This correction will be correct only for this chart; an adjacent chart may have a different correction. Always check both the datum and the correction for *any* chart you use.

Modern paper charts always state the correction to be applied when plotting using a WGS84 position. An alternative method is to reset the GPS receiver to present the latitude and longitude to the datum used by the chart. If you do this, you need to remember to reset it if you change the chart. If you're plotting on paper, it should make little difference using the incorrect datum unless you are navigating solely by GPS in a close quarter's situation. Remember errors due to using the incorrect datum could exceed 200 metres (600 feet), so that if your approach channel is only 100 metres (300 feet) wide, you could end up on the rocks!

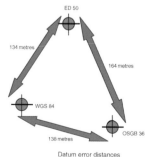

Datum error distances

Electronic Charts

Electronic charts are copies of paper charts. There are two types of electronic charts:

- *Raster charts* which are faithful reproductions of paper charts that have been scanned to produce the electronic copies. These will have the same datum as the paper chart scanned.
- *Vector charts* which are based on paper charts but enhanced to give 'added value' and if necessary have their datum changed so that all vector charts are WGS84 'compatible'.
- *Electronic chart plotters* use vector charts, so no correction is required.
- *Personal computers* may use either raster or vector charts, so the user needs to set or allow for the relevant map datum.

Chart Errors

There's a general feeling that electronic charts, because they are of the computer age, must be correct. *This is a dangerous assumption because it is simply not true.*

Before we explore the reasons for these errors, just study the three accompanying illustrations. All are of the north coast of the island of Ibiza,

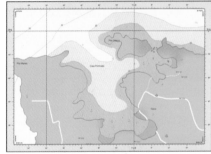

in the Mediterranean. All are different versions of modern electronic charting. The up-to-date Navionics chart shows an island at the head of the bay. The very old C-Map chart shows no island and the latest C-Map chart shows the reality. Compare all these with the Google Earth photograph.

So the first 'rule of using electronic charting' is 'caveat emptor'.

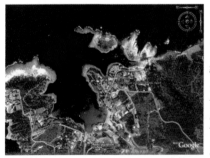

When was the Survey Carried Out?

UK Hydrographic Office charts always have a source diagram on the chart. This shows both how and when the survey was carried out. Unfortunately not all charts have a source diagram and no vector charts I have seen have them either. Raster charts will if the original paper chart has one.

Vector charts will generally show the date of issue of the paper chart on which it was based, but this chart may well use cartography several hundred years old. Some charts are still based on Captain Cook's surveys and some Pacific Islands are reported to be up to 8 miles out of place.

Note how this area around the Channel Islands in the English Channel was surveyed mostly in the nineteenth century!

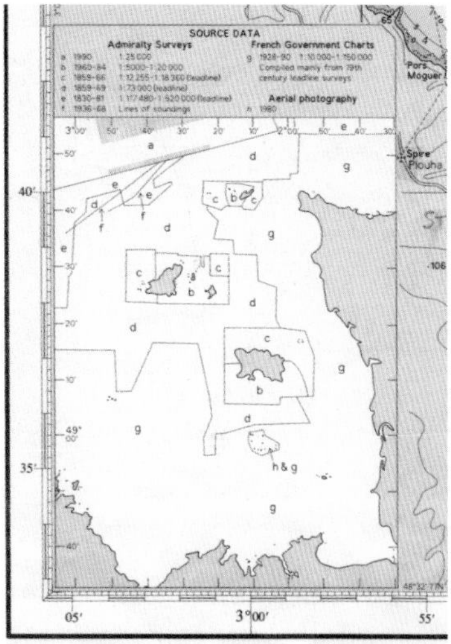

Surveying is very expensive and will not be carried out just to satisfy the 'leisure market'. Where commercial

UK Hydrographic Office source diagram

needs dictate, up-to-date surveys will be carried out, but this may be only in the channels and approaches used by commercial shipping, leaving the shallower areas unsurveyed by modern means.

In the United States of America, 40% of the shoreline has not been mapped since 1960. Around half of the soundings were carried out by lead line survey prior to 1940 (US Federal Advisory Committee Report 2007, which stated 'depending on the boater's location … can render these charts slightly to grossly inaccurate'). Any electronic chart of the US will be based on these charts.

Who Drew the Chart?

You cannot assume that the chart's publisher carried out the original cartography. The source diagram above shows that although it's from a British Admiralty chart, some of the cartography is French. One can probably make an assumption that not all cartography will be as good as that of the major seafaring nations.

Who Copied the Chart?

Vector charts rely on people to not to make errors when compiling the chart, but naturally errors will occur.

Chart Corrections

Chart corrections are published regularly to correct known errors and to introduce new data. The user is responsible for either buying updated charts or incorporating the updates when published.

Common Sense

This all sounds very alarmist, but common sense and the use of as many navigation tools as possible must be used at all times. It's an old axiom that groundings occur not because the navigator is uncertain of his position, but because he is sure that he knows where he is but is wrong! Navigators uncertain of their position navigate very cautiously.

The accompanying illustration from the chartplotter of a cautious navigator (an ex airline pilot) shows the planned inbound route to Figeuira da Foz, in Spain. The red 'Xs' are his planned *waypoints*. The red *track line* shows where the chartplotter thought they were, but of course, our cautions navigator followed the buoys, leading lines and the 'lie of the land' to complete a successful arrival. But if it were night or foggy, another 'gung ho' navigator would have ended on the rocks.

The longitude was correct, but the latitude had an error of about 0.15 minute – about 300 metres (900 feet). Was this a datum error, a cartographic error, a vectorisation error or a GPS error? Who knows but it could have ended up as a shipwreck whatever the cause.

Chart Scale

Charts vary according to the area that they cover and hence the detail they contain.

The scale of a chart is given as a ratio; one unit of length on the chart represents very many units of length on the Earth's surface. So a chart scale of 1:1 000 000 means that 1 inch or 1 centimetre on the chart represents 1 000 000 inches or centimetres on the Earth's surface.

The scale chosen for use in any particular circumstance depends on the detail required. You could not enter a harbour using a 1:1 000 000 scale chart; you would probably use a chart with a scale of 1:10 000 or 1:5000.

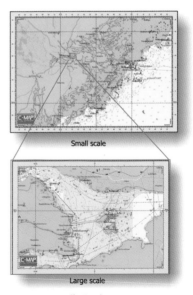

Small scale

Large scale

Chart scale

- A *small-scale* chart covers a *large area* and has a high-scale number (say 1:1 000 000) (one divided by one million is a small number).

- A *large-scale* chart covers a *small area* and has a low-scale number (say 1:5000) (one divided by five thousand is a larger number and therefore larger scale).

Ideally, you would have a small-scale chart of your cruising area and large-scale charts containing more detail for the harbours and anchorages. In fact, you may need charts of an intermediate scale as well. I, personally, don't buy charts by scale. I look at individual charts and their detail and buy what I want to suit my needs.

Measuring Latitude and Longitude

There will be a grid of latitude and longitude superimposed on the chart. This grid will be in degrees and minutes, as appropriate to the scale of the chart. To obtain the latitude and longitude of any point, we need to compare the position of this point with the grid. Several different tools may be used to do this, and navigators have their own preference.

Using dividers is the only correct method where the meridians are not parallel, such as on a conical projection. However, on such charts the errors using a parallel rule or course plotter will be very small unless the chart's scale is small. If the meridians look parallel, then the error will be too small to be significant for normal navigation.

We'll look at how we would measure the latitude and longitude of a special mark (buoy) near Sydney, Australia, whose position is 34° 06.548′S, 151° 24.962′E.

Using a Parallel Rule

Measuring Latitude

The parallel rule is placed on the nearest part of the *longitude* grid and opened out to touch the point of interest. The position of the rule is adjusted so that one edge cuts a *latitude* graticule and the latitude read off.

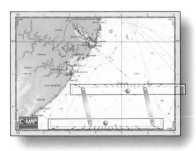

Measuring latitude with a parallel rule

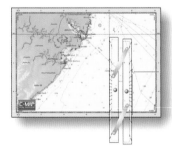

Measuring longitude with a parallel rule

Measuring Longitude

The parallel rule is placed on the nearest part of the *latitude* grid and opened out to touch the point of interest. The position of the rule is adjusted so that one edge cuts a *longitude* graticule and the longitude read off.

Using a Course Plotter

Measuring Latitude

The edge of the course plotter is placed on the point of interest and aligned so that the opposite edge or the plotter's grid is parallel with the *longitude* grid. The latitude is measured where the plotter's first edge cuts the *latitude* graticule.

Measuring Longitude

The edge of the course plotter is placed on the point of interest and aligned so that the opposite edge or the plotter's grid is parallel with the *latitude* grid. The longitude is measured where the plotter's first edge cuts the *longitude* graticule.

Using Dividers

Measuring Latitude

Place one point of the dividers on the point of interest and open them out so that the other point touches the *latitude* grid at its closest point. Move the dividers so that one point touches the same latitude grid where it has a graticule and read of the point's latitude.

Measuring Longitude

Place one point of the dividers on the point of interest and open them out so that the other point touches the *longitude* grid at its closest point. Move the dividers so that one point

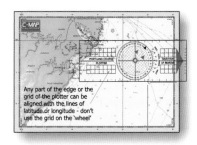

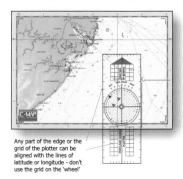

Measuring latitude with a course plotter

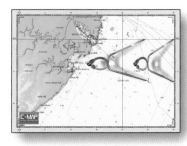

Measuring longitude with a course plotter

Measuring latitude with dividers

touches the same longitude grid where it has a graticule and read of the point's longitude.

Chart Symbols

Each charting organisation has its own standard chart symbols. They are all pretty similar and there's a new international standard set of symbols for electronic charting.

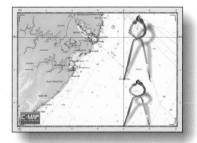

Measuring longitude with dividers

The geographical position is shown by the circle

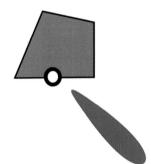

A lit navigation aid is shown with a magenta flash

Navigation marks

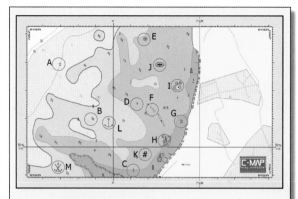

Some chart symbols

A	10 metres contour
B	3.9 metres sounding
C	0.0 metre sounding, that is, chart datum
D	Rock of unknown depth consider dangerous to surface navigation
E	Rock awash at chart datum
F	Area which covers and uncovers
G	Drying height of 0.2 metres
H	Rocks which cover and uncover
I	Rock which does not cover (height 1.3 metres)
J	Wreck of unknown depth dangerous to surface navigation
K	Foul ground – if you drop your anchor here it may become fouled
L	Recommended anchorage
M	Anchoring prohibited

The major hydrographic organisations publish books containing all the symbols that they use and many of the charts produced for leisure boaters have lists of chart symbols printed on their reverse. Most almanacs also contain a list of commonly used symbols.

Some heights and depths are shown inside brackets, such as (1.7). This means that it can't be put on the chart in exactly the correct place, as it would obscure the detail – they put it as close as possible and enclose it in brackets.

Some symbols are much bigger than their physical counterparts – they are out of scale. The geographical location of the symbol, a buoy, say, is shown by a small circle at the base of the symbol.

Lit navigation aids are shown with a magenta flash.

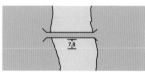

Clearance under a bridge

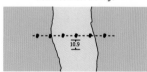

Clearance under a cable

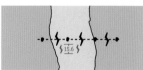

Safe clearance under a power transmission cable where published otherwise the actual clearance is shown in black

Vertical clearances

Symbols Depicting Dangers to Navigation

Certain symbols should be committed to memory, as you may not have time to look them up before you encounter an unmarked obstruction:

- Shallow water
- Rocks
- Wrecks
- Overhead cables
- Bridges with low clearance

If you are approaching a charted symbol you don't recognise, check what it means before you get too close.

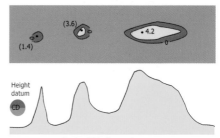

Rock which does not cover,
height above chart datum

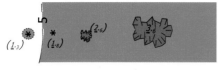

Rock which covers and uncovers, height above chart datum, where known

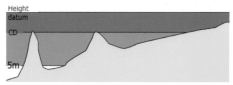

Rock awash at the level of chart datum

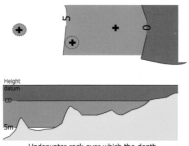

Underwater rock over which the depth is unknown, but which is considered dangerous to surface navigation

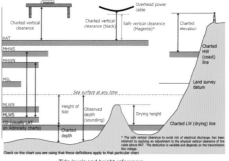

Tide levels and height references

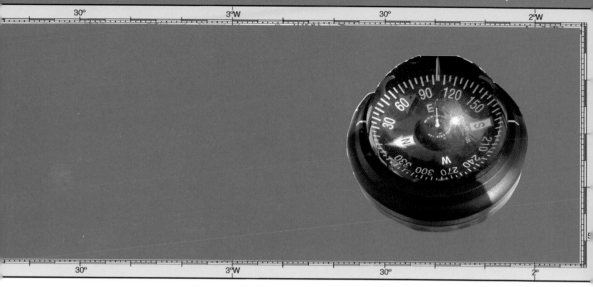

The Magnetic Compass

The Earth's Magnetic Field

Steering Compasses

Compass Deviation

Compass Correction

DIY Compass 'Swing'

Fluxgate Compasses

The magnetic compass has a magnetised pointer that aligns itself with the Earth's magnetic field. It, therefore, points towards the Earth's north magnetic pole and so allows the user to 'know where North is'.

The Earth's Magnetic Field

There are two aspects of the field which directly concern the compass needle:

- The horizontal component of the field determines the direction the needle points towards the poles. This is the useful part of the field and gives magnetic direction.
- The vertical component of the field forces the needle to tilt in a downward direction towards the nearest pole. This is the detrimental part of the field, which makes the magnetic compass unusable as it nears the magnetic poles. The angle of the field 'downwards' is known as 'dip'.

Steering Compasses

A steering compass is designed to be fixed in position on the boat and is used by the helmsman to 'steer' the boat on a compass course. It is mounted in a 'gimbal' so that the compass stays level, regardless of the heeling or pitching motion of the boat.

To best cope with the problems caused by the dip of the Earth's magnetic field, the magnet is suspended under the 'compass card' according to the hemisphere in which it is designed to be used. In fact there are three types of compass: Northern Hemisphere, Equatorial and Southern Hemisphere. In reality, I have a number of friends who have completed full circumnavigations on their yachts using a northern hemisphere compass and they reported experiencing no problems as a result.

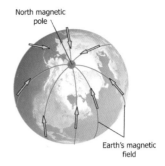

Earth's magnetic field

Compass needle aligns itself with Earth's magnetic field horizontally

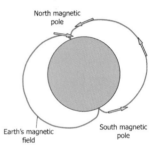

Compass needle aligns itself with magnetic field vertically

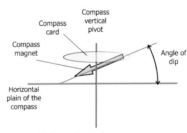

Northern Hemisphere compass

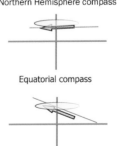

Equatorial compass

Southern Hemisphere compass

Compass Deviation

A boat is likely to have a magnetic field of its own, due to the magnetic materials such as its engine, incorporated into it. When the boat remains in a fixed position for some time, its own magnetic field becomes aligned with that of the Earth's magnetic field. When the boat is moved onto any other heading, the magnetic field experienced by the steering compass is a combination of the Earth's and the boat's fields and so the compass does not point directly towards magnetic North. This error is called 'deviation' and will vary in value as the boat's heading changes. Not only that, but also the error will vary as the boat heels, although this is difficult to allow for and is normally ignored.

Compass Correction

Compass errors should be measured and corrected. With possible errors as large as 30 degrees, relying on an uncorrected steering compass can result in dangerous navigational errors. Prior to electronic navigation, steering compasses were routinely checked and adjusted, if necessary. These days many boat owners rely on the electronic element of their navigation to take them to their destination and never even consider compass deviation.

   Commercial vessels have their compass corrected by professional 'compass adjusters'. Leisure boat owners can check compass deviation themselves and some 'leisure' compasses allow some simple form of correction. Owners of steel vessels need to take special precautions with their compass installations as the steel hull has a significant magnetic influence.

DIY Compass 'Swing'

It is pretty easy to measure compass error and the process is called 'swinging the compass'. Although the process used by the amateur will not be as accurate as when carried out by a professional compass adjuster, it will be entirely adequate for quantifying any major compass errors.

- Align the boat on a northerly heading using the steering compass.

- Using a hand-bearing compass in known position of minimum deviation, note the heading (to the bows of the boat).

- Continue the procedure noting both the steering compass and hand-bearing compass bearings every 30 degrees until you reach north.

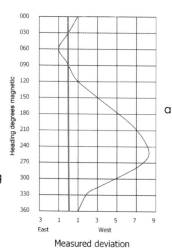

Measured deviation

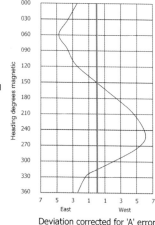

a

Deviation corrected for 'A' error

Magnetic course	Deviation (+ = west)
000	001
030	002
060	005
090	008
120	008
150	007
180	005
210	003
240	001
270	000
300	−001
330	000
360	001

Total 040
Average (A error) 3
Rotate compass 3 degrees eastwards

Measured deviation

Magnetic course	Deviation (+ = west)
000	−002
030	−001
060	002
090	005
120	005
150	004
180	002
210	000
240	−002
270	−003
300	−004
330	−003
360	−002

Deviation corrected for 'A' error

- Draw a deviation curve.
- If the curve sticks out more on one side of zero deviation than the other, the compass can be rotated in its mount to make the average deviation as close to zero as possible. This error is known as 'A' error.

Deviation of the Hand-Bearing Compass

Fixing bolts and slots, allowing limited adjustment of 'A' error

Adjusting compass for 'A' error

Compass deviation occurs due to the boat's magnetic effect where the compass is positioned, not due to any inherent compass problem. When using the hand-bearing compass, you should find a position in the boat where the boat's deviation is zero or a minimum. This is likely to be as far away from any magnetic material as possible. This could be in the bows or the stern depending on the position of the engine.

To check the deviation in any position, sight the hand-bearing compass on a distant but prominent landmark. Let the boat carry out a full 360-degree circle. If there is no deviation, the hand-bearing compass will maintain a constant bearing all the way around the turn. If the bearing changes, the maximum deviation is half the total change of bearing, though you won't know the actual deviation on any particular heading.

Correction for other errors by an amateur on a leisure boat compass is either not possible or not desirable. Knowing and allowing for any error is sufficient.

Very Large Errors Need to be Investigated

One motor cruiser I was checking had compass errors exceeding 30 degrees – entirely unacceptable. Someone had fitted a loudspeaker on the other side of the bulkhead in the cabin and only a few inches from the compass. Removing the speaker removed the deviation!

On another occasion the boat builder had mounted the windscreen wiper motor only 300 mm (one foot) away from the steering compass. As it wasn't practicable to move either, the large deviation had to be accepted and allowed for.

Fluxgate Compasses

Autopilots and radars need a compass input. This comes from a 'fluxgate' compass, which consists of coils that measure the Earth's magnetic field electronically. There's no magnet in this unit, which is mounted remotely in a suitable position, and the output is sent to any unit or display needing magnetic heading information.

'No magnetic material' warning sign
Fluxgate compass detector

Positioning of the Fluxgate Compass

There are two basic requirements:

- a position of minimum motion due to pitch, heave and roll;
- a position on minimum magnetic deviation.

Fluxgate compass

Often these two requirements are in conflict. The first condition is usually achieved by fitting the fluxgate in the after third of the hull's length. The next best is the middle third and the least desirable is the forward third. However, this latter position is often found to be the area of least deviation! Compromise is required.

Note: The detector must be mounted 'athwart ship' and may need to be mounted *either* on the forward *or* aft side of the bulkhead – check the installation instructions.

Autopilot Compass Swing

The fluxgate compass is swung in a special calibration procedure, detailed in the operating manual for the autopilot. Although not a perfect procedure, it is likely to result in the removal of most of any deviation but should be followed by a normal compass swing for the autopilot display and a deviation curve or table provided.

Magnetic course	Steer binacle	Steer autopliot
000	001(+1)	359(−1)
030	032(+2)	028(−2)
060	065(+5)	059(−1)
090	098(+8)	091(+1)
120	128(+8)	121(+1)
150	157(+7)	148(−2)
180	185(+5)	177(−3)
210	213(+3)	208(−2)
240	241(+1)	239(−1)
270	270(+0)	270(+0)
300	299(−1)	301(+1)
330	330(+0)	331(+1)
360	001(+1)	359(−1)

Combined deviation card

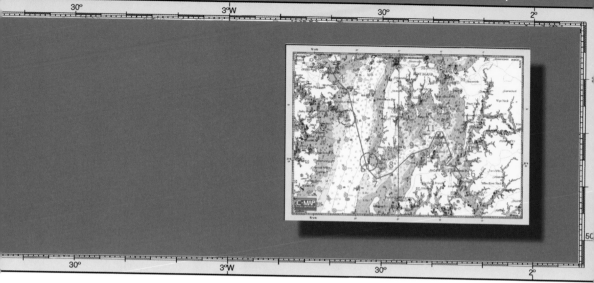

Constructing a Route

Using Second-Hand Waypoints

Loading the Route into the GPS

Constructing a Route on an Electronic Chartplotter or PC

These days we probably think of a route defined by a series of *waypoints*, places to which we wish to go in the process of getting from one place to another.

The term waypoint is relatively modern, stemming from the need to find the latitude and longitude of a point so that we could then enter it into a navigation receiver's processor via a keyboard. When navigation was less sophisticated, we would put some lines on the chart and plot our position to endeavour to keep as close to track as possible. There was no need to extract and write down any latitude and longitude at all unless we were using a sextant.

These days we should be able to enter into the 'navigator' the coordinates (latitude and longitude) of any position that is on our 'way'. These are the waypoints.

The process will differ according to the type of 'navigator' we are using; GPS receiver or GPS chartplotter.

Using Second-Hand Waypoints

You can buy books of waypoints. Also pilot books, almanacs and boating magazines list waypoints. I never use waypoints that I have not plotted myself, and I never join waypoints from a list to form a route, unless I have inspected the area on a recognised chart, paper or electronic. What is the point of using waypoints, the author of which states that you use them at your own peril and that they should not be used for navigation?

A Route for Use with a GPS Receiver

Here, our starting point is a paper chart on which we can draw a complete route. It may not have sufficient detail in areas where we are close to danger, but we can see the whole route on one sheet.

Choose your route so that it is as short as possible, *but* avoids passing too close to any possible hazard. It's possible that you may have to adjust the route when you look at smaller scale charts where the route needs to be inspected more closely.

Do not use the actual position of navigational marks as waypoints. GPS can be so accurate that you might collide with the buoy, and if other navigators also use the same mark, you may collide with their boat. Aim 100 metres or so off.

The small scale chart used for the overall plan

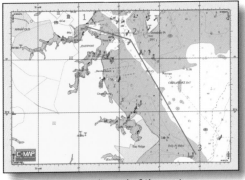

Let us construct a route from Annapolis to St Michaels in the Chesapeake. We'll need a chart with a scale of around 1:1 25 000 for the overview and charts of a scale of around 1:2 500 for each end where we need more detail.

Starting at Annapolis we can put the first three waypoints on the large-scale chart, before moving to the small-scale chart to add the next seven waypoints.

The Annapolis end of the route

Now we'll need to use the large-scale chart for St Michaels to put the rest of the waypoints in place.

The St Michael end of the route

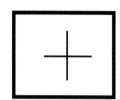

Waypoint symbol

Route from Annapolis to St Michaels –
An overview

Route plan				
Annapolis - St Michaels				
WAY PT.	Latitude north	Longitude west	Distance	Track (T)
1	38 58.61	076 28.78		
			0.95	106
2	38 58.35	076 27.71		
			2.25	150
3	38 57.21	076 27.34		
			1.9	155
4	38 57.20	076 27.34		
			1.5	132
5	38 56.20	076 25.97		
			7	166
6	38 49.92	076 23.65		
			1.5	137
7	38 48.55	076 22.54		
			1.6	072
8	38 48.92	076 20.86		
			2.5	048
9	38 50.68	076 18.28		
			1.6	072
10	38 51.35	076 16.73		
			1.6	025
11	38 52.71	076 15.28		
			0.6	090
12	38 52.71	076 14.82		
			2.4	158
13	38 50.56	076 13.71		
			1	226
14	38 49.94	076 14.36		
			1	102
15	38 49.64	076 13.11		
			1.4	150
16	38 48.67	076 12.44		
			0.35	199
17	38 48.32	076 12.53		
			0.35	184
18	38 48.18	076 12.67		
			0.3	131
19	38 47.71	076 12.35		
			0.6	233
20	38 47.32	076 12.93		
		Total distance	30.4	

Route plan Annapolis – St Michaels

Once you have a safe route, mark the waypoints and determine their coordinates. There's no standard symbol for a waypoint, as there are other navigation details, such as position. Many navigators, however, use a square with a cross in the middle.

Measure the distance and direction of each leg and note these down on a 'plan'. It's a good idea to use a printed 'pro forma' for this, or on the route-planning page of your navigation logbook. You will end up with something like this.

Note that I put the waypoints on every second line, so that the distance and tracks are on the intermediate lines separating each waypoint. This makes it easier to read than some other systems.

Loading the Route into the GPS

The first thing to remember is that 'rubbish in = rubbish out'. We all know how easy it is to miss-key numbers using a keyboard. The only way of checking you have entered the route correctly is to check the route once it has been entered, and this is where the 'tracks and distances' table comes in.

Once the route is loaded, go to the GPS display that shows the distances and tracks between each waypoint. Some early GPS sets didn't allow this and were potentially dangerous. Check that the distances and tracks tally with your 'paper' plan. You may see a constant error in the tracks. This will probably be because you have measured 'true' directions on the chart, but have told the GPS to display bearings in 'magnetic', or *vice versa*. Any discrepancy must be investigated and usually it's because a latitude or longitude has been miss-keyed, or misread from the chart.

This procedure is mandatory if you wish to avoid potential disaster, but *see the next paragraph*.

Problems with Some GPS Receivers

When you try and review the route on *some* GPS receivers, you may find what appears to be a serious discrepancy in the leg distances. This is because the distances shown, on these sets, are not the *leg* distance but the *running totals*! This is unhelpful to the conscientious navigator, who is now required to carry out additional arithmetic to ensure that the route has been correctly entered.

Constructing a Route on an Electronic Chartplotter or PC

This is much simpler than the previous example, but potentially more dangerous because of the small size of the screen. This danger can be avoided by constructing the route on paper charts first and then transferring it to the chartplotter, or by meticulously zooming in and out and panning backwards and forwards on the plotter or PC screen, as you construct the route.

The courses shown are the actual 'leg-to-leg' bearings

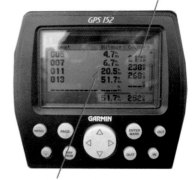

These distances shown are in fact the running totals, not the distance of each leg, as one should expect to be displayed on the 'route review page'

Reviewing the route

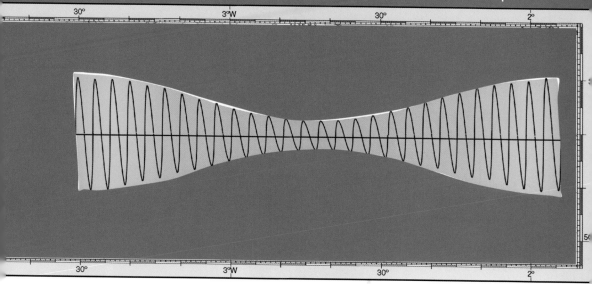

Tides

Tidal Heights

Tidal Flow

Finding the Value of the Tidal Flow

Tidal Heights

The Earth and its oceans are subject to the tidal 'pull' of the Sun, Moon and planets. As far as navigators are concerned, it is the combined effect on the level of the surface of the seas that is of interest and this is primarily affected by the relative positions of the Sun and the Moon, whose gravity causes a bulge of water in the direction of the gravitational pull. The bulge is stationary, but the rotation of the Earth on its axis makes it appear that the bulge rotates around the Earth once every 24 hours. At this point, most of the books suddenly draw in a second tidal bulge opposite the first to give us our 'two tides a day' without any explanation.

A simple way to view this is that the Earth gets 'pulled' by the gravitational effect as well, but being solid, it gets pulled as one lump, whereas the oceans, being fluid, are distorted. Thus the Earth is moved within the distorted 'oceans' to give two tides a day. The bulge closest to the Sun is of a slightly different shape to that on the opposite side of the Earth so that successive tidal 'curves' are slightly different in shape and height.

39

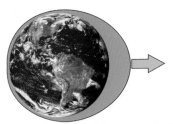

The gravitational pull on the fluid oceans – a 'bump'
is pulled towards the gravitational source.

The gravitational pull on the solid earth – the whole
earth is pulled towards the gravitational source within
the 'oceanic bump'

How gravity causes two tides a day

In the open ocean, the tidal effect is very small, with a daily rise and fall of sea level due to gravity of approximately only 0.3 metre or 1 foot. However, where the proximity of land channels the tidal bulge, the rise and fall is increased and values of up to 15 metres (nearly 50 feet) are seen in some parts of the world.

The Mediterranean and other 'inland seas' and Great Lakes are considered to be 'tide free' although there is a small tidal effect. Trieste, in the Mediterranean, for instance, has a spring tidal range of just over a metre, whereas other parts of the 'Med' have ranges of only 0.3 metre (1 foot).

Spring Tides

When the Earth, Sun and Moon are on the same axis, the gravitational effects are at maximum and the tidal bulge is largest. As the Earth spins within the bulge, the sea level rises as the bulge approaches, reaches a maximum and then falls to a minimum about 6 hours later. The difference between the height of the high water and the height of low water, the *range*, is a maximum and this is known as a *spring* tide and occurs twice a month.

Large tidal bulge

Spring tides occur at New and Full moon

Spring tides

Because of inertia effects, spring tides happen a couple of days after the time when the Sun, Moon and Earth are in line. Spring tides occur, then, a couple of days after the New Moon or the Full Moon are seen.

Neap Tides

When the line joining the Earth and Moon is at right angles to that joining the Earth and Sun, the gravitational force on the Earth and oceans is minimum and so the gravitational bulge is a minimum also. The tidal range at this time is minimum and these 'lower tides' are called *neap* tides. Neap tides are associated with 'Half Moon', but inertia also affects this; so neap tides occur around 2 days after the first and second 'Half Moon'.

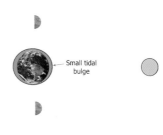

Neap tides occur at times of 'Half' Moon

Neap tides

Tides change from spring tides to neap tides and back to spring tides over a 14-day period. The heights of a spring and neap tides vary throughout the year, the highest springs being associated approximately with the equinoxes in the spring and autumn; hence the term 'spring' tides. The lowest neaps are associated approximately with the solstices, the origin of the term neap being unclear but probably originating from the old English 'nepflod' used to describe the lowest high waters.

Tidal Range

Whether a tide is neap or spring (or an intermediate) is determined not by the height of high water but by the difference between the height of high water and the next (or preceding) low water. This is called the *tidal range*. Spring tides have a large range and neap tides a small one.

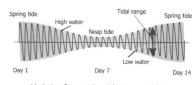

Variation from spring tide to neap tide

The mean sea level remains roughly constant. At springs, the high water is very high and the low water very low, while at neaps, the high water is much lower and the low water much higher.

With the introduction of international standards for electronic charting, there is a trend for all hydrographic authorities to adopt the same terminology for tide levels. Although there are many different tidal height definitions in the United States of America, such as MLW (mean low water), MLLW (mean lower low

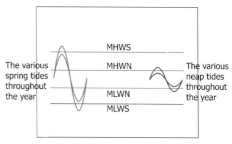

Mean high and low water levels

41

water), MHW (mean high water) and MHHW (mean higher high water), which are still used on paper charts, the following are understood and becoming more common:

MHWS – mean high water springs   MHWN – mean high water neaps

MLWS – mean low water springs   MLWN – mean low water neaps.

Approximately, spring tides will be 25% greater than the mean range and neap tides will be 25% less than the mean range.

The Tidal 'Day'

As the Earth spins on its axis once every 24 hours, one might expect that the tidal 'day' would also span 24 hours. In other words, there would be two high waters in 24 hours, each being 12 hours apart. In fact successive high waters are about 12 hours and 25 minutes apart, so why is this?

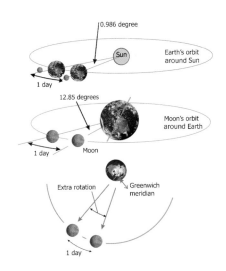

Tidal 'day' is longer than 24 hours

Each 'second' high water occurs when that meridian faces the Moon (ignoring inertia effects). As the Earth moves along its orbit around the Sun and the Moon moves in its orbit around the Earth, this takes longer than 24 hours. The average 'extra time' between each second high water is around 50 minutes, but varies between 29 minutes and 1 hour and 26 minutes, because the angular rotation of the Earth around the Sun is not constant. Therefore, on an average, each high water is 12 hours and 25 minutes later than the last.

High Water Time

For any given location, the time of day when high water springs occurs is roughly constant. Likewise the time of the local high water neaps is also roughly constant.

Look at your local tide tables to see what these times are for your home port, and you then have a valuable planning tool.

For instance, in the UK's Solent, high water springs occurs at approximately 12 midnight and 12 noon. High water neaps occur at approximately 6 a.m. and 6 p.m. If you look in your diary to check the 'phase' of the Moon, you can get a reasonable idea of the time of high water, which can be useful if you don't have your tide tables to hand.

Chart Datum (Nothing To Do with Map Datum – the Reference for Latitude and Longitude)

For navigation purposes any water depth has to be referenced to a common datum for it to have any meaning. Most authorities use a datum called *chart datum (CD)*, which to all intents and purposes is the lowest astronomical tide (LAT) *for that length of coastline or that particular port.*

In the United States of America, this is LLW (lowest low water). However, MLLW may be used as the tidal datum for tidal curves in the United States of America and is not as low as lowest astronomical tide. In the United Kingdom, it is called CD or LAT, and in France it is 'Niveau zero' the lowest equinoctial tide.

The reason for using LAT is that there will always be at least the depth shown by the soundings, even at low water. Any higher datum will inevitably mean that sometimes there will be less water than the charted depth.

There is a common misunderstanding that chart datum is constant for the whole of a chart, but this is not so. Coastal effects could cause the lowest astronomical tide to be significantly different at two places close together on the same chart.

The table shown indicates the chart datum associated with different places along part of the UK's Kent coast. They are all referred to the UK Ordnance Survey datum situated at Newlyn, Cornwall, in the United Kingdom, this point being the UK's reference for sea level for all UK maps. The table indicates that there is a 2.34 metres difference in LAT along this stretch of coast.

Tidal levels referred to datum of soundings							
Place	Latitude (N)	Longitude (E)	Heights in metres above datum				Datum and remarks
			MHWS	MHWN	MLWN	MLWS	
Dover	51° 07'	1° 19'	6.7	5.3	2	0.8	3.67 metres below ordnance datum (Newlyn)
Deal	51° 13'	1° 25'	6.1	5	2	0.8	3.40 metres below ordnance datum (Newlyn)
Richborough	51° 18'	1° 21'	3.3	2.7	0.3	0.1	1.33 metres below ordnance datum (Newlyn)
Ramsgate	51° 20'	1° 25'	4.9	3.8	1.2	0.4	2.58 metres below ordnance datum (Newlyn)
Broadstairs	51° 21'	1° 27'	4.6	3.7	1.3	0.4	2.35 metres below ordnance datum (Newlyn)
Margate	51° 24'	1° 23'	4.8	3.9	1.4	0.5	2.50 metres below ordnance datum (Newlyn)

Chart datum information as found on UKHO charts

It's also worth noting the significant difference in spring and neap tides from place to place along this 35 miles coastline.

Using Chart Datum

Now we have a load of definitions to think about, what use are they? We need to be very careful when checking depths, heights and clearances under obstructions as not all hydrographic authorities use the same standards. Because commercial shipping is changing over to the use of electronic charts, the International Maritime Organisation introduced a new standard in 2006/2007. Beware, then, not only the 'make' of chart, but also when it was issued. You must check the notes on any chart, or the current list of symbols and abbreviations to see what standard applies to the charts you are using.

Charted depths below chart datum (LAT) are added to the tidal height to find the actual depth (the sounding) at any given time.

Drying heights above chart datum (LAT) are subtracted from the tidal height to find the depth at any given time – *by the very nature of the beast, this depth may actually be above the present water level.*

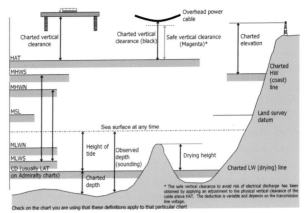

Tide levels and height references

The Tidal Curve

All major ports, known as *standard ports or reference ports*, have 'tide tables' prepared for them by various authorities. These are projected for at least 12 months in advance and often considerably longer. They are based on historical records which allow real tides to be matched to astronomical data. Formulae are then deduced that match the data so that projections may be made for future dates. Generally, the 'match' is good, but differences will always occur. Tidal data cannot take account of transient metrological conditions. Atmospheric pressure of 10 millibars (0.03 inch of mercury) above average (1013.2 millibars–29.92 inches of mercury) will force the water level down by 0.1 metre (4 inches) and conversely the water level will rise by the same amount if the pressure is 10 millibars below average. A strong wind blowing from a constant direction for several days can also raise or lower the water level considerably and it is not unknown for meteorological conditions to change the predicted tide level by as much as 0.5 metre and sometimes considerably more.

It could be argued, then, that the pursuit of super-accuracy in tidal calculations is not appropriate for *most* situations. However, in calm conditions, access across a shallow sandbar may be made using carefully calculated 'height of tide' at low speed with little clearance under the keel – preferably on a rising tide in case you get it wrong.

Secondary Ports

It is uneconomical to have tidal curves and full data for all harbours and anchorages. These 'other' harbours are known as *secondary ports* and are listed with tables of differences from a standard port. Using these differences, the times of high and low water and their heights can be calculated from the tide times of the standard port and its tidal curve.

Standard port			0000	0600	0100	0700				
Port dirty			and 1200	and 1800	and 1300	and 1900	5.1	2.6	1.5	0.1
Secondary ports				Time differences				Height differences (in metres)		
Place	Latitude	Longitude	High	Water	Low	Water	MHWS	MHWN	MLWN	MLWS
Nice Harbour	43 26	035 45	−0035	−0020	−0010	−0020	+0.4	+0.2	+0.1	+0.0
Hope Cove	43 33	036 21	+1005	+0055	+0020	+0010	−0.2	−0.1	+0.0	+0.0

Secondary port differences

Electronic Tidal Curves

Without any doubt, these are the easiest and quickest ways to obtain tidal height information. Because each provider may use data from different authorities, there may be apparent discrepancies between different products. The differences may seem large at first glance, with times of high water sometimes differing by as much as half an hour, but when you look at the heights involved, these show that they are less than 0.05 metre (less than 2 inches) apart at the same time, so in reality there is a little difference between them.

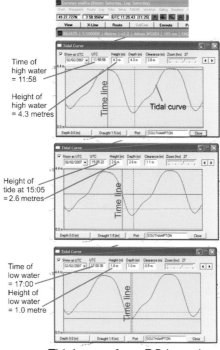

Tidal curve from PC based navigation software (*seaPro*)

All chartplotters have tidal curves these days, as do many of the PC navigation software packages. There are several tidal programmes available for hand-held computers and some ordinary GPS receivers are able to display tidal curves.

In these, having selected the day in question, you only need to scroll the curser along the 'time line' of the curve for the predicted tidal height to be displayed. Many can be programmed with the draft of your boat to give an instant reading of the clearance under your keel. You will need to consult your instruction book to see how to do this with any particular system.

Paper Tidal Curves

Standard Ports

Different authorities present their data in different ways. Although the curves will be similar, the method of extracting the actual heights for times other than high or low water will differ and may not be obvious to someone used to a different method.

The 'Rule of Twelfths'

In the open sea and along coasts which do not alter the natural shape of the tidal curve (a sine wave) very much, a good rule of thumb that needs nothing except the heights of high and low water is the 'rule of twelfths', though you may find a calculator handy.

This assumes that in the first hour after high water the level falls by *one twelfth* of that tide's range from high water; after the second hour it has fallen by *three twelfths*; after the third hour, *by six twelfths*, the fourth hour by *nine twelfths* and the fifth hour by *eleven twelfths*.

This is the principle used by clocks and watches that indicate the state of tide. It follows that these work only if the tidal curve is close to 'normal' in shape.

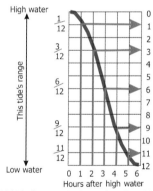

Multiply the range by the number of twelfths to get the fall from high water

The 'rule of twelfths'

UKHO Method

Tidal curves for ports around the United Kingdom are often far from symmetrical and don't lend themselves to 'rule of thumb' methods of calculation. The UKHO has developed an excellent and simple method of obtaining the height of tide at any time. For full details of this method see Appendix 3.

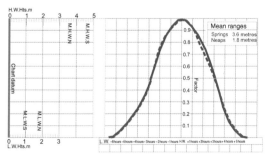

UKHO style tidal curve for port somewhere

The French (SHOM) Method

The French take a very different approach, which works well for 'smooth' curves, but doesn't take account of 'lumpy' curves, as does the UK method. To allow for neaps and springs, each 'tide' is given a factor, with 100 representing the equinoctial tides above and below mean water level, whose factor is zero. This gives an immediate idea of how 'springy' or 'neapy' the tide is. A graphical solution is used to calculate the height of tide at any given time which takes into account any differences in time taken for the tide to rise, compared with how long it takes to fall (the skew of the tidal curve), but doesn't allow for any 'bumps'. This method is easy, but accurate only for smooth curves. (see Appendix 3 for full details).

Secondary Ports

The UKHO tidal curves make it very easy to adapt the curve for the standard port into the curve for the secondary port, using a graphical solution. With practice the procedure is quick and easy, although to be honest, many yachtsmen are put off using it, maybe because they are striving after unnecessary accuracy.

The French (SHOM) method allows calculation of tidal heights for secondary ports.

Most of the others require mental gymnastics if you need to know tidal heights at times other than high or low water.

For detailed instructions, see Appendix 3.

Calculating the Depth of Water

The principal reason for using tidal height data is to check if the water is deep enough for your boat or that there's sufficient clearance to pass under a bridge or cable. You can use 'electronic' tidal curves if you have them – that's the easiest way – or you'll need to do it all on paper.

Depth in Which to Anchor

It's a good idea to consult the chart for the general depths and to see if there are any rocks or shallow bits, but you won't be using chart datum or soundings.

What you need to know is how much the tide will fall from *now* until the *time of low water.*

Add to this the *draft* of your boat and the *safety allowance* you would like under your keel, what the French call the 'navigator's foot' (pied de pilote), and that's it! That's the minimum depth in which to anchor.

If you are staying over more than one tide, remember to check the lowest low water over the period that you expect to anchor. If it's getting more 'springy', your under-keel clearance will get less each tide.

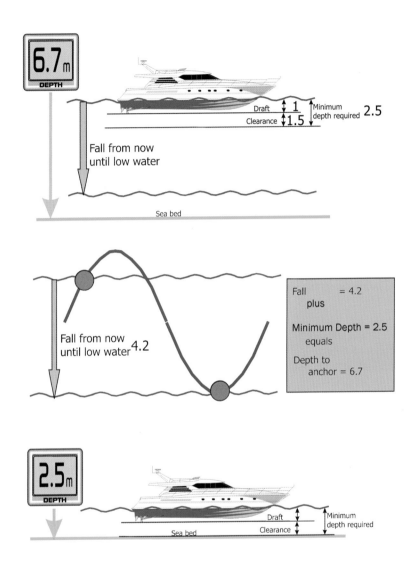

Depth to anchor

Calculating the Depth of Water

For this you will need to consider the chart datum and the charted depth or drying height.

   Add the charted depth to the height of tide or subtract the drying height from the height of tide to find the depth of water.

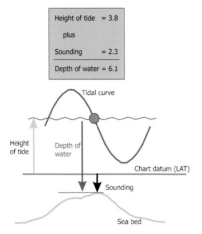

Height of tide = 3.8

plus

Sounding = 2.3

Depth of water = 6.1

Calculating the depth of water
with a sounding

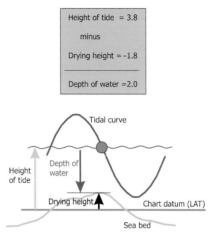

Height of tide = 3.8

minus

Drying height = -1.8

Depth of water = 2.0

Calculating the depth of water
with a drying height

Is There Enough Depth of Water to Allow My Passage?

Here we use the depth calculated as above and compare it with the draft of the boat plus the safety allowance. If the depth is greater, we're fine, if it's less we can't proceed. Often we need to find the earliest and latest times we can pass over a sandbar into or out of a harbour. For this we need to know between what times the depth of water will be at least our draft plus allowance.

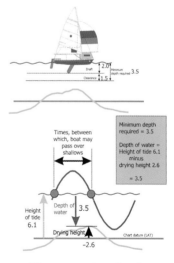

When can we enter or leave?

Can We Get Under the Bridge?

In this calculation we use a different *datum*. If we used LAT, there would *always* be less clearance than that shown on the chart, except at lowest astronomical tide, LAT or its equivalent. This would be potentially dangerous. Until 2006, different authorities used some form of 'higher high water' – MHWS in the United Kingdom or MHW in the United States America. In France they used mean sea level. Now all *new* charts should use highest astronomical tide (HAT). Check what standard your chart is using if you don't have much clearance.

The charted clearance under a cable takes into account the electrically safe clearance, that is there's an allowance for how far the spark can jump! A high-voltage cable will have a bigger allowance than if it were low voltage.

This calculation is a little more complicated because the clearance is above HAT but the water level is above LAT. All we have to do is *add* the *difference* between *HAT* and *LAT* to the charted *clearance*, subtract the *height of tide* and we have the *clearance above the water* level. Ok, so a picture is worth a thousand words; well, here's the picture. And yes it's safe to go under. We can, if we need to, find the times between which we can pass safely under the obstruction.

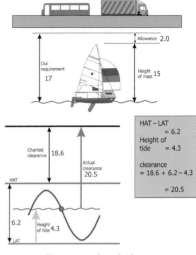

HAT – LAT
= 6.2
Height of
tide = 4.3

clearance
= 18.6 + 6.2 – 4.3
= 20.5

Clearance under a bridge

Tidal Flow

The Speed of the Bulge

The Earth spins within the tidal bulges, giving the appearance that the bulges rotate around the Earth. At the Equator, the 'ground speed' of the Earth, due to its spin, is approximately 1000 miles per hour and at 45 degrees North and South, this speed is approximately 700 miles per hour. At 45 degrees latitude, high tide rushes towards us from the east at 700 miles per hour. Makes you think, doesn't it?

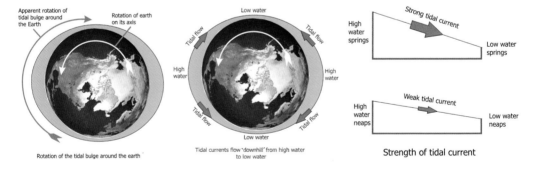

Where there is a constriction to the flow of the tidal bulge, such as in the English Channel, this speed is considerably modified with the bulge taking around 6 hours to travel from Dover to Falmouth, a distance of about 250 miles, a speed of around 40 miles per hour.

What Causes the Tidal Currents?

The prime mover is the difference between the heights of tide at any two places. Water wants to flow downhill, which is exactly what it does. Thus you would expect there to be zero current at high water as the tide changes direction. This is called *slack water*. The same applies at low water.

However, this is not always the case, as there may be another current flowing as well, which will add to, or subtract from, the tidal current. Consider a river estuary: There may be a river current of three knots, flowing towards the sea. The *flood tide* may be flowing at two knots upstream, so although the tide is rising, the current is still flowing out to sea at one knot – opposite to that which you might expect.

The speed of the tidal current will be strongest at spring tides and weakest at neaps because the slope of the water is steeper at springs as the high water is higher and the low water lower.

Currents due to Eddies

Less intuitive is somewhere such as the Channel Islands, situated in the English Channel. Because the Channel Islands are situated in a large bight and the English Channel becomes very much narrower at this point, a large, rotating, tidal eddy is set up which at times runs counter to the current set up directly by the tidal bulge. In parts of this area, slack water occurs at 'half tide up' and 'half tide down'!

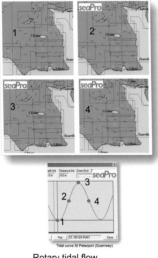

Rotary tidal flow

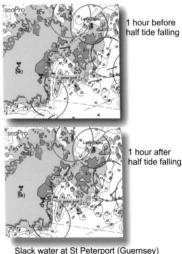

1 hour before half tide falling

1 hour after half tide falling

Slack water at St Peterport (Guernsey) occurs at half tide up and half tide down

Eddies in a channel, close to the shore can cause the tidal current to reverse some time ahead of 'slack water'. Knowledge of these is very useful if you are trying to 'cheat' the tide.

Currents Caused by Wind

Tidal currents can be modified by wind. A strong wind blowing for some time sets up a general movement of the surface water due to friction. This wind driven surface current can counter or add to the tidal current, and needs to be considered when considering the tidal *set and drift* (the tidal effect on the boat) when planning a passage.

Wind Against Tide

Where a wind driven surface current is running counter to the tidal current, a significant change in wave shape will occur. This effect is known as *wind against tide* and can make a relatively calm sea change abruptly as the tide 'turns'. Where the tidal current is large and the wind strong, conditions can change from *uncomfortable* to *dangerous* very rapidly.

Currents in the Open Oceans and Inland Seas

Because the difference in water level due to the tide is usually very small, generally there's no significant tidal flow. However, this doesn't mean that there are no currents. Currents may be seasonal, such as the North Atlantic's Gulf Stream, in which case they can be predicted long term, or wind driven, in which case they change from day to day.

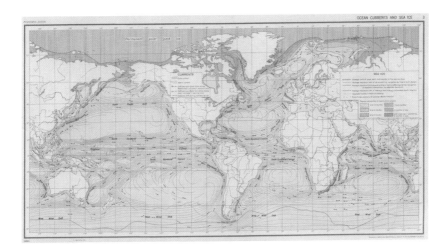

Even though the difference in tidal heights is small, a restriction to the flow by such things as islands can cause acceleration to the small tidal current to a much larger value that needs to be taken into account. Amongst other places, this effect can be seen in parts of the Mediterranean Sea.

Finding the Value of the Tidal Flow

Various hydrographic departments will have built up a database of tidal flow at specific points during the tidal cycle for neap and spring tides.

Tidal Diamonds

These specific points are shown on charts as a diamond with a letter of the alphabet inside the diamond. These are known as tidal diamonds.

A table is included with specific values of tidal set (spring and neap values) and direction for each hour before and after high water at the stated reference port at the position of each diamond.

The lettered diamonds indicate the position for each set of tidal stream data

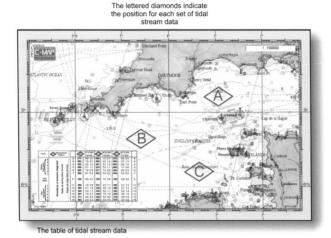

The table of tidal stream data

Tidal diamonds

Hours		Geographical Position			◆ Ⓐ	50°13'.00N 2°55'00W		Ⓑ	49°38'.00N 3°22'00W		Ⓒ	49°10.00N 4°37'00W		
Before high water	6	Directions of streams (degrees)	Rates at spring tides (knots)	Rates at neap tides (knots)	−6	074	0.9 0.4	064	1.3 0.7	079	0.8 0.4			−6
	5				−5	082	1.5 0.7	065	2.3 1.2	085	2.7 1.3			−5
	4				−4	085	2.0 1.0	067	2.7 1.3	083	2.8 1.4			−4
	3				−3	089	2.1 1.1	070	2.3 1.1	082	1.7 0.8			−3
	2				−2	090	1.6 0.8	071	1.5 0.8	083	0.6 0.3			−2
	1				−1	096	0.7 0.3	062	0.4 0.2	084	0.4 0.2			−1
High Water					0	256	0.6 0.3	256	1.2 0.6	258	0.9 0.5			0
After high water	1				+1	266	1.8 0.9	251	2.2 1.1	268	2.3 1.2			+1
	2				+2	265	2.1 1.0	246	2.6 1.3	266	2.7 1.4			+2
	3				+3	264	2.2 1.1	244	2.2 1.1	262	2.8 1.4			+3
	4				+4	267	1.5 0.7	248	1.6 1.8	264	2.0 1.0			+4
	5				+5	271	0.4 0.2	259	0.4 0.2	270	0.8 0.5			+5
	6				+6	062	0.5 0.3	062	0.9 0.4	070	0.4 0.2			+6

Tidal stream data for each hour before and after the time of high water

We can see that there is only one reference port for any tidal flow table. The time of high water is not for the position of the diamond or even for the nearest port. The reference port may not even be on that chart. It is chosen by the hydrographer to give the most helpful and representative reference time of high water for the area under consideration.

Tidal Atlases

Many charts, pilot books and almanacs contain tidal atlases showing the tidal currents. A small chart has tidal flow arrows marked on it, together with the speed of the current. There is 1 chart for every hour, so there will be 12 charts, enabling the user to estimate the tide at any time in the tidal cycle.

The actual values used in tidal atlases are obtained using the tidal diamond data.

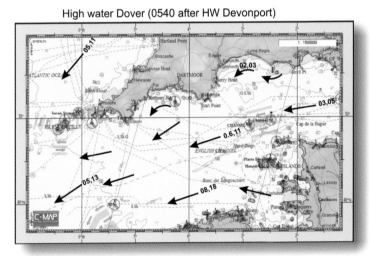

High water Dover (0540 after HW Devonport)

Tidal stream atlas for western English Channel

Tidal Diamonds Versus Tidal Atlases

Which should you use, diamonds or atlases? If you need to know the information for a particular point such as when diving, use the diamond. For planning or general navigation, it's normally easier to use an atlas.

Tidal Speeds and Directions

Generally, there will be two values for the tidal speed, one for spring tides and one for neap tides. Often these are shown without a decimal point, so 23 is not twenty-three knots, but two point three. Where two figures are shown, the greater is for spring tides, the lesser for neaps and a mental interpolation is sufficiently accurate – in other words, a good guess.

The direction of the tidal arrow is the direction of the flow. Tides, unlike winds, flow *to* a compass point, so a north-westerly tide is flowing towards the north-west. On many tidal atlases the boldness of the arrow signifies its speed.

Each chart will be named for a specific hour before or after high water at the reference port. The currents shown are the average for that particular hour, and apply from half an hour before until half an hour after the nominal time.

Tidal Reference Port

The reference port for tidal atlases need not be for any port particularly close or even within the charted area. What matters is that high water times and tidal range are readily available and that ideally it's in the same time zone so that silly errors can be avoided. The reference port is always stated on the tidal atlas.

You could, and mostly would, be approaching a destination, whose *standard* port for tidal *height* calculations is different from the *reference* port used to obtain the tidal *flow*. This is normal, but sometimes confusion arises as to which information should be in use.

The rule is simple: use the reference port shown on the tidal atlas for the tidal flow, and the standard or secondary port shown on the tide tables for the height of tide.

Tidal Flows on Chartplotters

The electronic charts supplied with modern chartplotters usually have a database that allows the tidal flow to be shown in real time on the plotter's screen. The arrows often have different colours to represent different speed bands. Some allow the tidal flow at different times and the flow at a specific point to be displayed.

Tidal Flows on PC Charting Software

Tidal flow arrows can be shown on many brands of chart-plotting software. Often, by placing the curser at a particular point, the actual value can be shown for that point.

Tidal flow arrows on C-Map max
electronic chartplotter

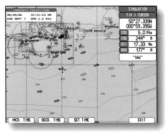

Actual value of tidal flow at the curser.
Using the keys to increment or decrement
time in one-hour steps, the change in flow
can be investigated. A specific time can also
be set.

New time

Change keys
Investigating the flow C-map max

Toolbar allows time to be changed so that
tidal flow can be investigated

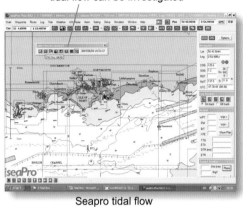

Seapro tidal flow

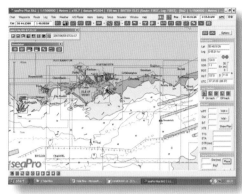

Tidal flow arrows on Seapro PC plotting
software

Tidal flow at a specific point and time
Seapro

It is of help when planning a trip to 'scroll' the displayed chart backwards and
forwards in time to see how the tidal flow changes during the day for any date. This is
much the same as looking at the various plates on a tidal atlas, but with the computer
doing all the high water time calculations for you.

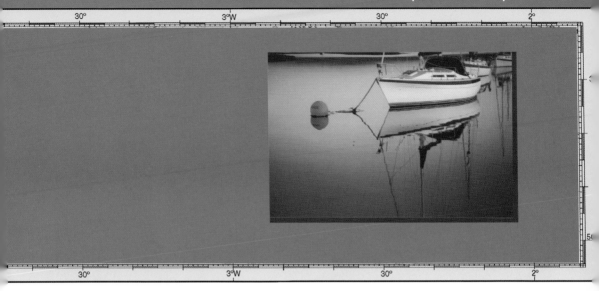

Boat Speed

Speed over the Ground

Speed Through the Water

Measuring Speed Through the Water

Log Errors

There are two sorts of boat speed: speed through the water and speed over the ground.

Speed over the Ground

Speed over the ground (SOG) is measured by GPS and is the total sum of boat speed, tidal effect and wind effect. It is covered in Chapter 1.

Speed Through the Water

This is the resulting speed through the water due to the power of the engine or sails overcoming the drag of the boat in the water and in the air. It is a measure of the boat's performance and is used for traditional chart work and navigation.

Measuring Speed Through the Water

A 'transducer' measures the flow of water past the hull and sends the information to the speed instrument.

Modern speed transducers consist of a paddlewheel protruding slightly below the hull into the water. Any flow of water past the paddlewheel causes it to rotate and the electronics counts the number of revolutions in a given time. This allows the electronics to calculate boat speed and distance travelled. The 'log' as the transducer is known, often incorporates a water temperature transducer as well. Some earlier logs had a little propeller-shaped transducer mounted behind a small fin. The traditional 'trailing log' used a propeller on a long length of line, let out behind the boat, and a mechanical counter that displayed distance travelled. The navigator had to calculate his own speed.

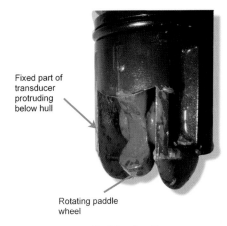

Fixed part of transducer protruding below hull

Rotating paddle wheel

Paddle wheel log

Logs with no moving parts, using the 'Doppler shift' in frequency to measure boat speed have been tried but did not find favour.

Log Errors

The log will read the correct speed (and distance) only if the speed of the water flowing past the hull is the same as the boat's speed through the water. Seems pretty obvious, but because of friction, the layer of water close to the hull gets slowed down. In reality of course, it's the boat that's moving through the stationary water, but the effect is the same – The boat drags some of the water close to the hull along with it.

To allow for the friction effect, the log must be calibrated.

Calibrating the Log

Traditionally, the boat would have covered an official 'measured mile' in both directions and the log distance would have been averaged to calibrate the log.

Today, the GPS 'speed over ground' can be observed and the predicted tidal flow used to calibrate the log.

Two Ways to Do It:

Slack Water

- Calculate the time of slack water.
- Proceed to a buoy or post so that you can check that the tide is slack by observing its 'wake'.
- Adjust the log speed readout to agree with the GPS SOG.

Slack water

Any Other Time

- Use the tidal atlas (or chartplotter tidal flow facility) to find the tidal flow at the current time.
- Find a buoy or post and motor into tide to make the boat stationary relative to the post. SOG should be zero and the boat speed should indicate the strength of tide, which should agree with the prediction.
- Motor at your normal cruising speed and adjust the log speed to agree with the GPS SOG, allowing for tide; that is if you are motoring into a tide of 2 knots, the boat speed should read 2 knots more than SOG.

Depth Sounders

How They Work

Depth Units

Calibration

Depth Alarms

False Echoes

Fishfinders

The depth of water in which the boat is floating is measured by a depth (or echo) sounder.

How They Work

A transponder sends a pulse of energy downwards from the bottom of the boat. This pulse is reflected by the seabed and returned to the transponder, which is now listening for the return. The time taken for the pulse to travel from the boat to the seabed and return can be translated by the depth sounder's electronics into the depth of water below the transponder. This depth is displayed on the screen of the depth instrument.

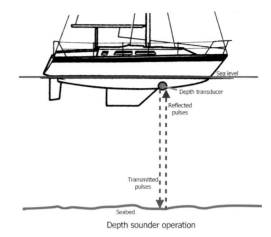

Depth sounder operation

Depth Units

Depth sounders can be set to fathoms (one fathom equals 6 feet), feet or metres. Ideally, the units displayed should be the same as those of the navigation chart you're using.

Calibration

By default, the depth displayed will be the depth below the transducer, which is of no use to anyone. Normally, you'll be able to adjust the display to show the depth below the keel or the depth below the waterline. This is known as an offset.

Many users set the depth to 'depth below the keel'. However, if you wish to use the depth sounder as a navigation tool, it's much better to set the offset so that 'depth below the waterline' is displayed. This is the actual depth of water. If you want to know the depth below the keel, all you need to do is to subtract the draft of the boat and this becomes an automatic action.

How to Calibrate Your Depth Sounder

- Moor your boat in fairly shallow water, preferably with a seabed that is firm and of constant depth.

- Lower a weighted line over the side until the weight just touches the bottom (the line just goes slightly slack).

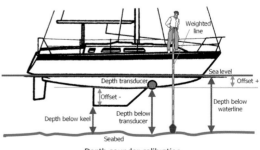

Depth sounder calibration

- Note the point on the line where it enters the surface of the water (if you're quick in hauling the line back up, you'll see where the line becomes wet).
- Measure the 'wet' length of the line.
- Adjust the depth sounder offset so that the unit displays the actual depth of water.
- If you prefer to have 'depth below the keel', set the offset so that the unit displays the actual depth minus the draft of the boat.

Depth Alarms

Many depth sounders allow you to set up one or more audio alarms to warn you that the water is getting shallower (or deeper) than you would like so that you can take appropriate action.

False Echoes

Reflections from turbulence may cause a false shallow depth to be indicated or the signal may be lost altogether, causing the display to flash on and off.

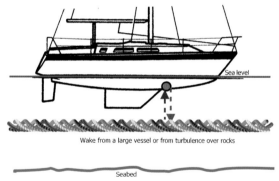

Wake from a large vessel or from turbulence over rocks

Seabed

False echo

Fishfinders

Fishfinders use these 'false' echoes to indicate the presence of fish and expert fishermen can even identify the type of fish on very sensitive units.

Fishfinder display

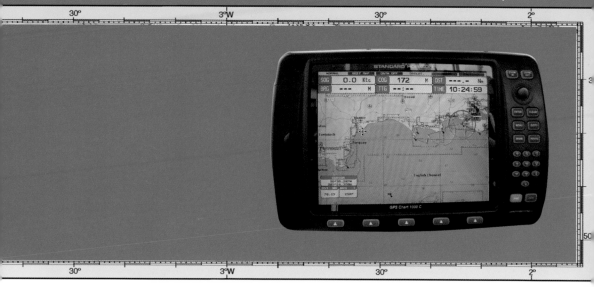

Finding Position

GPS

A GPS receiver will give us our present position in the form of Latitude and Longitude, so that we won't know where we are until we plot this on a chart.

Active Route

If we have constructed and activated a route, or used the 'Go-To' or MOB functions, our GPS set will give us distance and bearing to the next waypoint and also any cross-track error. The cross-track error is how far left or right we are from the direct line between the position that we activated the route (or pressed the GO-To or MOB keys) and the next waypoint (or place we want to go to or MOB).

The distance to go, bearing to waypoint and cross-track error can all be used as position lines to plot on a chart to make fixing our position easier. Remember though these three types of position line are GPS based and if that is in error, our position lines are inaccurate and could be dangerous. As usual, we should always use as many different navigation tools as possible.

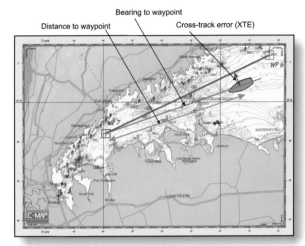

Distance to waypoint

Bearing to waypoint

Cross-track error (XTE)

Bearing and distance to waypoint and cross-track error

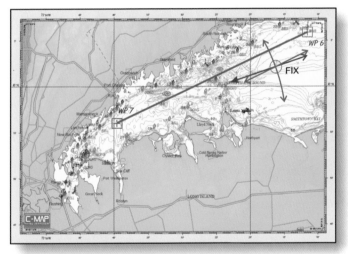

GPS fix – brg, dist and XTE

Other Methods

In the age of satellite navigation, it might seem illogical to use anything other than GPS as a means of finding ones position. Indeed, one can argue that to proceed to sea without GPS could be construed as negligent.

However, in Chapter 1 (GPS) and Chapter 2 (Charts) we have seen that errors are possible. On top of this the failure of a single GPS receiver or its power supply can deprive us of this vital piece of equipment.

The most obvious alternative to GPS is visual navigation or pilotage. If you are passing a named buoy or obvious landmark, you know where you are. There are other well-tried methods as well.

Position Lines

A position line is a line on the chart or earth's surface on which you must lie. There are a number of means of obtaining position lines and different means may be mixed to 'fix' your position.

Hand-Bearing Compass

A small hand-held compass can be aligned with a geographical feature and the magnetic bearing from the boat to the feature measured.

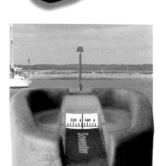

In order to plot this bearing on a paper chart, it must be converted to a bearing of the boat from the feature by adding or subtracting 180 degrees. This is known as the reciprocal bearing. The magnetic bearing must also be converted to a true bearing by adding the variation if East or subtracting if West. Using a Portland type plotter, all the conversion can be achieved on the plotter, rather than in the head or on paper. It is very difficult to achieve an accuracy of better than 5 degrees due to the motion of the boat. A legs-apart stance to brace your body is advised.

Single Position Line Using a Hand-Bearing Compass

In this case, a bearing from a boat to a lighthouse is measured as 277 degrees magnetic using a hand-bearing compass. The magnetic variation is 8 degrees East, so the true bearing is 285 degrees. Using the plotter as described in Chapter 2, it

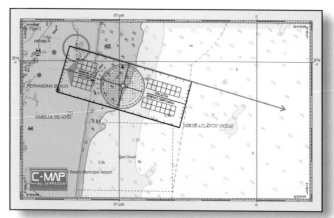

Single position line using a hand-bearing compass

is aligned with the base of the lighthouse symbol. The boat must lie somewhere on the position line drawn along the plotter's edge (shown in red).

Single Position Line on a Depth Feature

Here, we are crossing the English Channel. If we suddenly find that our depth, corrected for height of tide is between 1.6 and 2.7 metres, we must be somewhere along this very narrow depth feature, so we have an excellent single position line.

Single Position Line from a Transit

A transit is the visual alignment of two geographical features. If these features are aligned, you must be exactly on a position line joining them. It is the most accurate form of position line available. A transit may be the alignment of two natural features or the alignment of two deliberately placed navigation marks provided for safe navigation through a hazard-

A single position line derived from a linear depth feature

strewn area. In the latter case, the most seaward of the two marks is lower than the most landward one to ensure that you know which way to turn should you wander off the alignment. Official transits marked on a chart always have their directions given in degrees True.

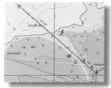

A position line derived from being on a 'transit'

Single Position Line Derived from Radar

Radar can allow us to measure both distance and bearing from a geographical position. Bearing is the least accurate and should not be relied on unless you have nothing better. Range (distance) is much more accurate. A distance from your boat to a feature as measured by radar will provide a curved position line, so you will need a pair of compasses to draw this on your chart.

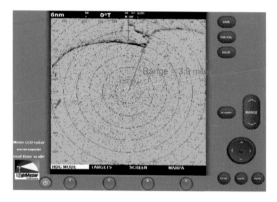

Radar range position line

Fixing Your Position Using Position Lines

Fixing your position using position lines should normally consist of three lines, with an angle between each line of 60 degrees for best accuracy, though this is often not possible. Features chosen should be unambiguous, easily identified both on the chart and on the skyline. If you are under way, measure the bearing that changes most slowly first (the one nearest ahead or astern) and the bearing that is changing most rapidly (the one nearest abeam) last. The time that you take the last bearing is the time of the 'fix'. Your position (at the time of the fix) is where the position lines intersect. The convention is to

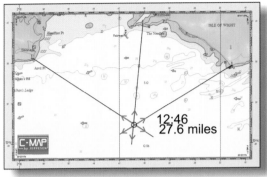

A three position line fix

draw a circle around this position, enter the time of the fix and the distance log reading at that time. Using the standard convention, anyone looking at your chart will have all the data needed, without having to look at your written logbook.

Errors in Position Lines

A big advantage of visual and radar position lines is that you are not relying on the accuracy of the cartography to avoid hitting the land. The land is where you or your radar sees it, not where the GPS or the mapmaker tells you where they think it is.

The position given by your position lines is correct in relation to the land, though it may not tally with the latitudes and longitudes shown on your chart – This is important if your charts have large errors, as some do. If your chartplotter shows that your boat is travelling merrily over the land, but your eyes show you to be safely floating on the water, which are you going to believe? Just have a look at the trace from this chartplotter.

It is very difficult to achieve an accuracy of better than plus or minus two and a half degrees when using a hand-bearing compass on a boat at sea. This will lead to errors of

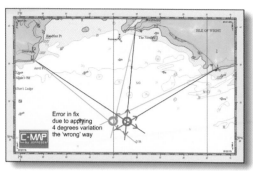

Error due to incorrect variation	Possible error in fix

±800 metres at 10 miles range from the feature, 400 metres at 5 miles and 250 metres at 3 miles, respectively.

Instead of the position lines intersecting at a point, you'll get a 'cocked hat'. The size of the cocked hat will give an idea of the accuracy of the fix.

The green polygon shown on the accuracy diagram is the area in which you might lie with a plus or minus two and a half degree error in all three bearings.

In particular, avoid the application of variation in the wrong direction, otherwise large errors can occur.

Transits

There should be zero error when the position line is based on a transit and hence a perfect fix results from the intersection of two transits.

Radar

The error of a position line based on a radar range should be no more than 1% of the range, though identifying the exact position of the geographical feature may not be so easy. Radar bearings are prone to error due to the alignment of the antenna, the width of the radar beam, the difficulty of identifying the feature and the application of deviation and variation, so should be used with caution.

How Far Can You See?

Because of the curvature of the earth's surface, the distance to the horizon, which is determined by your eye level, is possibly not as far as you might think. From an eye height of 2 metres it's only a little over 3 miles! Therefore, a buoy beyond 3 miles won't be seen, though in fact most buoys

Eye height	Distance to horizon	Eye height	Object height	Distance to horizon	Object height
(metres)	(N miles)	(feet)	(metres)	(N miles)	(feet)
2	3.11	7	2	3.11	7
4	4.40	13	4	4.40	13
6	5.39	20	6	5.39	20
8	6.22	26	8	6.22	26
10	6.96	33	10	6.96	33
15	8.52	49	15	8.52	49
20	9.84	65	20	9.84	65
50	15.56	163	50	15.56	163
100	22.00	325	100	22.00	325

Add the *distance to horizon* for your eye height to *distance to horizon* for the charted height of the object to obtain the distance it should be visible.

For a light, use this or the charted visibility, which ever is least.

Visible distance

are too small to be recognised from even this short distance. An object beyond your horizon can still be seen if its highest part is high enough to project above the horizon.

The things that determine how far away any object will be visible are:

- The meteorological visibility – Is it foggy?
- How big it is – Is it actually large enough to be discerned by your eye?
- Your eye height – If you are standing on top of a hill, you can see further.
- How high the object is – Is it high enough to project above your horizon?
- At night, how bright the object's light is?

Nautical almanac's provide tables of distance to the horizon for different eye heights and different object heights. Charts detail the heights of terrain, vertical structures such as chimneys and the heights of lights. They also show the visibility of lights in standard atmospheric conditions. Experience tells you how far away you can discern a buoy, typically no more than a couple of miles at most.

When All Else Fails

If you know where you started from, the course you have been steering, the distance you have travelled, you can deduce where you are. This is called 'deduced reckoning' or 'DR', often called 'ded reckoning' or more frequently 'dead reckoning' – Take your pick.

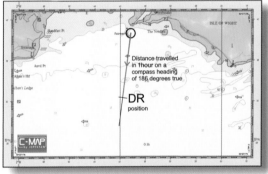

Dead reckoning position

If you're in tidal waters, then by applying how far the tide will have carried you while you've been travelling, you can estimate where you now are. Unsurprisingly this is known as 'estimated position' or 'EP'.

This method has been used since navigators started roaming the seas and is surprisingly accurate. Using this method, it's unlikely that you'll become terribly lost, provided that your compass and log have been properly calibrated. You'll almost certainly be no more than 10% of your logged distance run from your actual position.

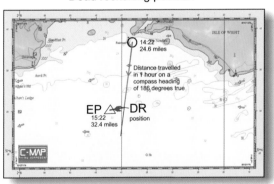

Estimated position

The chances are that you'll be much closer, so don't deride this method.

EP and DR are covered fully in Appendix A.

Chartplotters

An electronic chartplotter is a navigation instrument that displays the position of the boat superimposed on an electronic chart. You will find an electronic chartplotter simulator on the Wiley Nautical website at www.wileynautical.com

The boat's position is determined by a GPS receiver. The GPS receiver may be part of the chartplotter, with either an internal or external GPS antenna. Alternatively, the chartplotter may be supplied from a separate GPS receiver.

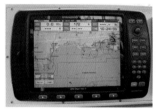

An electronic chartplotter

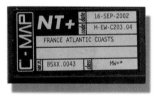

Chart data card

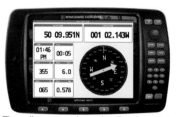

The yellow arrow shows the direction to follow

The waypoint is 0.356 miles distant and you will arive in 3 minutes

The waypoint is now dead ahead
(alligned with the red line, which allows for tide and leeway)

Turn boat to follow 'highway'

The electronic chart is supplied on a data card that is plugged into a card slot in the chartplotter. The electronic cartography may be provided by the chartplotter's manufacturer or by a third party provider. Ensuring accurate and up-to-date cartography is a large undertaking and some may consider that a large, well-funded specialist provider may be more accurate than a smaller provider's wares. Most chartplotter manufacturers stick with one provider, but some allow the use of several.

What Can a Chartplotter Do?

Tell You Where You Are

The first and most obvious thing is to display the boat's position on the chart so that you know where the boat is at any time. There are caveats here – See GPS errors in Chapter 1 and chart errors in Chapter 2. There are no source diagrams on electronic charts, although they may refer to the cartography on which they are based or at least the date of the source chart. That gives no idea at all of the date of the surveys, which may well have been in the 19th century.

Allow You to Construct a Route

You can construct a route that you would like the boat to follow. Here, there's another warning. Unlike a car's 'satnav', which is supposed to know where the roads are and will confine the route to known roads, there are no roads at sea. Ask the chartplotter to plan a route between two points which have land or rocks in the way, *it will direct you to run aground*! As detailed in Chapter 4, you must inspect the route thoroughly after you have constructed it.

Allow You to Follow a Route

Having constructed your route, you can follow the progress of the boat along the route to get you where you wish to go. This can be done in several ways:

- Steer the boat to keep as close as possible to the route as drawn on the chart.
- Allow the autopilot to follow the route automatically, although I don't approve of this method. Although this is the normal practise on airliners, there are several dangers on small craft. The navigator is never really aware of the compass course followed and so compass errors can pass undetected. The helmsman/navigator is removed from the close control of the boat and becomes less involved in its safe operation.
- Use one of several other displays available on the chartplotter to keep on track such as the highway or compass.

Allow You to Go Direct to Any Geographical Point

Chartplotters normally have a 'GO TO' function. If the cursor is placed over the point that you wish to go to and the you press the 'GO TO' key, a single leg route is set up giving you near instantaneous instructions of how to get there.

Place the cursor on your destination

Select 'CURSOR' in the 'pop-up' window

'Pop-up' window   HIGHWAY soft key
'Pop-up' window will show distance and
bearing to new destination

Select 'HIGHWAY' soft key to
display highway

Turn boat to follow 'highway'
or 'compass'

Allow You to Estimate the Height of Tide

Many chartplotters allow the tidal curve for a
specified point to be displayed. There will be
a number of tidal stations within the database,
signified by a special logo on the chart. If the
cursor is 'hovered' over the logo, the curve can
be displayed.

Allow You to View the Tidal Flow

Many chartplotters are able to display the tidal
flow in real time. Both the size and colour of the arrows
vary according to the strength of the current.

Tidal curve for a designated point

Man Overboard

Most chartplotters have a 'man overboard', key. This
operates much like the 'GO TO' function, except that when
you press the 'MOB' key, the geographical point at that
instant is the point to which you wish to go. It is very worth

Tidal flow arrows (red = strong)

while you experimenting with this function – It won't send any alarms to anybody.

Remember! The position shown for the casualty does *not* take into account any tidal
drift. You will have to look down tide for the casualty. A 1 knot tide will cause a drift of

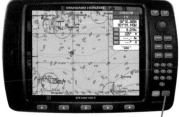

Press Man Overboard (MOB) button

Distance and bearing to MOB

This tells you that MOB has been activated

Track of boat   MOB position   ZOOM IN

Boat position

1. Press any key along bottom
2. Press key under NAV

Position of MOB   Red line is your COG (course over ground)

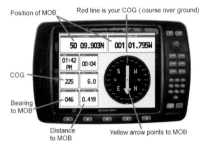

COG

Bearing
to MOB

Distance
to MOB   Yellow arrow points to MOB

Start turning the boat (preferably into tide)
to make the yellow arrow point to the top
of the screen

Continue the turn

The MOB is 0.356 miles distant and you will arive in 3 minutes

The MOB is now dead ahead
(alligned with the red line)

150 metres (170 yards) over a 1 minute period. Look at the chart page to find the
direction of drift.

Other Functions

There are many other functions available, so do read the user's manual for full details.

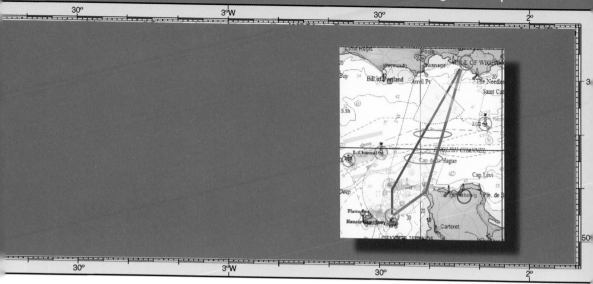

Passage Planning

You should have a plan for any passage you intend to make.

This plan can range from a quick look at the weather and tides for a short passage you've made many times before to a detailed written plan for a longer, open water one. The basic plan can be made well in advance, with only a check of the weather being required just before you start the passage.

The planning process has two stages. Firstly, you need to consider the broad picture – an 'overview', then you need to consider the plan in detail.

Overview

Look at the entire passage on a small-scale chart, preferably a chart that covers the complete route and consider the following:

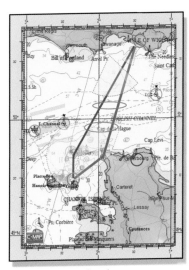

Overview

- Are there any tidal constraints at departure, destination or port of refuge?

- Best route to make best use of tidal streams and available navigation aids.

- Large-scale charts for passage and possible alternative ports.

- Shipping lanes and traffic separation schemes.

- Sunrise and sunset times (light identification times).

- Charted depths which might give a progress check.

- Draft outline plan, note distance and likely passage time.

Tides and Tidal Streams

- Note the times and heights of HW and LW at departure and destination.

- Time of HW and range at reference point for tidal atlas and tidal diamonds.

- Identify limiting depths and fast streams causing tidal gates, correcting plan as necessary.

Tidal Gates:

Needles favourable June 30th 23:00 until July 1st 06:00

Alderney Race favourable July 1st	*11:00 – 17:00*
Guernsey June 1st	*12:00 – 17:00*
Marina open HW +/–3 hours	*18:00 – 23:59*

Tidal gates

Navigation Aids

- Visibility of lights. Coverage of local radio stations for forecasts. Area of coastguard coverage. VHF channels. Racons (buoy with a radar beacon).

Yarmouth to Needles	6.0 miles
Needles to Alderney race	61.0 miles
Alderney race to Guernsey	23.0 miles
Total Distance Yarmouth to Guernsey	90.0 miles
Planned cruising speed	6.0 knots
Estimated time en route	15.0 hours
Needles to start of Westbound traffic lane	26.0 miles
Needles to start of Eastbound traffic lane	38.0 miles

Alternative destinations:
Cherbourg, available at all states of tide and in all weather.

Alderney. Ok but must not be swept passed by tide. Untenable in strong NE wind.

Outline plan

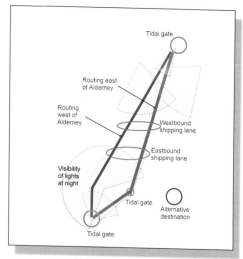

Key to overview chart

Detailed Plan

At this stage you can investigate the plan in more detail and if there are strong tidal streams and tidal gates you will need to keep refining the plan as you home in on the best departure time – what's known as an iterative process.

I'll Outline My Way of Doing This

- Using the initial approximate time the trip will take, I juggle any tidal gates to come up with a departure time. This may entail compromise.
- Knowing the departure time, I need to see what the actual tides are on the way to get much more accurate route timings. I use the tidal atlas for the trip, having checked the time of high water used by the atlas for the departure date and a strip of paper on which I can mark the length of the route to the same scale as the tidal atlas. I mark along this route hourly marks for my estimated boat speed. This allows me to move from page to page of the atlas to estimate the tide at the point I expect to be at that time. Sounds complicated? It isn't, as a look at the diagrams will reveal.

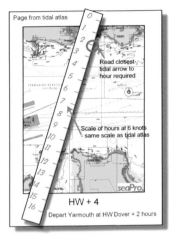

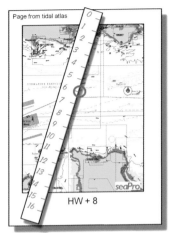

Tide at 2 hours from Yarmouth   **Tide at 3 hours from Yarmouth**   Tide at 6 hours from Yarmouth

- I make a table of the actual tides experienced for each hour along the route, as shown. I include more detail than absolutely necessary at this stage, but it saves work further along the process. Knowing the total distance to be covered is 90 miles, looking at the distance run column, I can see that the ETA at Guernsey will be a little after 16:00, say 16:10.

The method of working out course to steer is shown in Appendix B and Appendix D.

- I can now refine my original plan with more accurate timings.

1. Ideal departure time
2. Estimated arrival time
3. Pilotage for departure port, destination and possible ports of refuge.
4. Open sea passages: Tracks, distances and methods of navigation.
5. Dangers: Distance off to pass, clearing lines.
6. Shipping lanes: Cross at right angles?
7. Ports of refuge: Good shelter? Tidal or other restrictions.
8. Fuel: Gals/hour – passage time – reserve (20%)?
9. Watch system
10. Food

Just Prior to Departure

Check the weather.

Don't keep the plan a secret; discuss it fully with your crew so that they understand your intentions and have confidence in their skipper.

Passage Planning – Procedure

If you work your way through the following procedure, you'll have a plan.

Preplan

How far to go?
How fast will you travel?
How long will it take?
Look at tidal streams.
When should you start/finish to make best use of the tides?
Look at tidal heights.
Are there any tidal height/stream restrictions at departure, alternates or destination?
Do these modify start time?
If these times are incompatible, where can you wait?
Read all pilotage notes (almanac/pilot book).
Prepare pilotage plans.
Prepare route plan – plot on chart(s) – check all tracks and distances.
Load route into GPS/plotter – check all tracks and distances.
Plan catering.
Plan watch roster.

For the Planned Day of Departure

Times and heights of relevant high/low waters – springs or neaps?
Label tidal atlas.
Times of sunrise/sunset.

To steer a constant heading for the whole cross-channed leg (the most effiecient way) the course to steer is obtained from considering all the tides (see Appendix D). The course to steer and the planned ground track is shown here.

Passage Making

The easiest way to illustrate how to go about navigation, when applied to passage making is to have a look at a

High Water Dover 00:20 BST

Hour	Tide		Tidal gain	Tidal loss	Ground speed	Running distance	ETA	
0	←	2.2	1.5		7.5	0	02:00	
1	←	1.6	0.4		6.4	7.5	03:00	
2	←	1.8	0.5		6.5	13.9	04:00	
3	←	1.7	0.4		6.4	20.4	05:00	
4	←	1.8	0.5		6.5	26.8	06:00	
5	←	1.5	0.3		6.3	33.1	07:00	
6	→	0.8		0.2	5.8	39.4	08:00	
7	→	1.5		0.5	5.5	45.2	09:00	
8	→	2.5		1.0	5.0	50.7	10:00	
9	↗	3.1		1.3	4.7	55.7	11:00	
10	↗	2.2		1.5	4.5	60.4	12:00	
11	→	0.8	0		6.0	64.9	13:00	
12	↙	1.5	1.5		7.5	72.4	14:00	
13	↙	2.2	2.2		8.2	80.6	15:00	
14	↙	1.7	1.7		7.7	88.3	16:00	
15	↙	2.0	2.0		8.0	96.3	17:00	

Total Distance Yarmouth - Guernsey 90 miles
ETA Guernsey 16:10 approx.

En route tide - Yarmouth to Guernsey 1st July 2007

real trip. This is my method, and others may do things a bit differently, but I'll tell why I do things my way as we proceed from Salcombe in Devon to Poole Harbour in Dorset.

Before We Start

This is a trip of over 100 miles, so at a cruising speed of around 6 knots, it'll take around 17 hours, so here, in the English Channel, where tides can be quite strong, we will have to endure going against the tide for some of the time. I use Seapro chart-plotting software which allows me to investigate the best time to leave, taking account of the tidal flow. Doing it manually, you'll need to take a look at the tidal atlas and decide the best time of departure to make best use of the tides. With a forecast wind of northerly

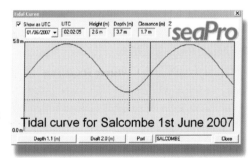

Yarmouth to Needles	6.0 miles
Needles to Alderney race	61.0 miles
Alderney race to Guernsey	23.0 miles
Total Distance Yarmouth to Guernsey	90.0 miles
Planned cruising speed	6.0 knots
Estimated time en route	15.0 hours
Needles to start of Westbound traffic lane	26.0 miles
Needles to start of Eastbound traffic lane	38.0 miles

Alternative destinations:
Cherbourg, available at all states of tide and in all weather.

Alderney. Ok but must not be swept passed by tide. Untenable in strong NE wind.

Outline plan

force 4, I hope that we should cruise at about 6.2 knots and Seapro tells me a good time to leave Salcombe is 03:00 BST, taking around 16 hours and 40 minutes to Poole entrance.

Salcombe has a shallow sandbar in the entrance with a least depth of 1.1 metres, so it's worth checking what depth will be available at 03:00. Salcombe's tidal curve shows that the tide will be rising and there will be about 3.7 metres over the bar at 03:00.

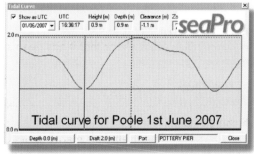

Poole Harbour entrance is narrow and the tide runs very strongly, so I need to ensure that we get there on the flood. We'll be getting there a little before high water, so that's ok. If we're a bit late, there's a high water 'stand' and I'll have a good couple of hour's leeway. If I'm very late, I'll have to anchor outside, which with a forecast wind from the north is fine.

Checking the tidal atlas, I see that the tide outside Salcombe starts to run to the east just after we leave. It starts to run against us halfway across Lyme Bay, where the tides are weak turning favourable again around Portland Bill, giving us a fair tide all the way to Poole. This confirms that Seapro has come up with a good answer.

Seapro also has given me the course to steer for each leg, their distances and bearings and the times. The method of

Moon rise 22:21   Moon set 05:26 (full moon)
Sunrise   05:05   Sunset 21:07

Depart Yarmouth	02:00
Needles	03:00
Start westbound shipping lane	07:30
Start eastbound shipping lane	08:00
Enter Alderney Race	13:00
Guernsey (St Peter Port)	17:00
Marina open	18:00
Marina closed	01:00

Skipper on watch	01:30 – 04:30
	07:30 – 09:00
	12:00 – 14:00
	15:00 – 18:00
Crew on watch	04:30 – 07:30
	09:00 – 12:00
	14:00 – 18:00

If strong wind against tide in Alderney race (3.0 knots)
Route via west of Alderney or change destination to
Alderney or Cherbourg

Final plan

doing this manually is given Appendix B. I can now draw the tracks on my navigation chart and check the distances and bearings. If I were entering this data manually into a GPS receiver, it's essential that I thoroughly check all the bearings and distances – rubbish in equals rubbish out. My system allows me to send the route directly from my laptop to my GPS, but I still need to check that it has been sent to the correct place.

On the Way

I don't mark the pages of my tidal atlases with the high water times. I have a card on which I can enter the times and heights based on HW time plus and minus half an hour, rather than HW time itself. This means that I can instantly see what page I should be looking at, just by reference to the clock and the card.

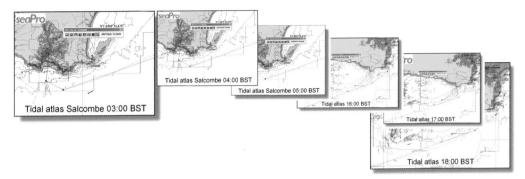

Tidal atlas Salcombe 03:00 BST

Tidal atlas Salcombe 04:00 BST

Tidal atlas Salcombe 05:00 BST

Tidal atlas 16:00 BST

Tidal atlas 17:00 BST

Tidal atlas 18:00 BST

We leave Salcombe using pilotage, rather than navigation (see Chapter 10), so apart from entering our departure in the log, I don't start my chart work until we reach waypoint number two. GPS is to be my main means of fixing our position, so I will be just plotting our GPS position on the chart every hour, with the occasional bearing to check the GPS. This way, should we loose our GPS or it becomes inaccurate, we will never be more than an hour away from the last reliable fix and it's from this position that I would start my 'traditional navigation' (see Appendix A). It often makes sense to base the time of the hourly fix on the changeover time of each page of the tidal atlas, rather than the 'top of the hour'. If I were travelling in a fast motor cruiser,

WP	BRG (T)	DIST	CTS (M)	Leg time	ETA DEST	WP Position
0						
1	187	2.8	192	0:29	03:29	50 11.21 N 03 46.24 W
2	117	2.1	121	0:19	03:49	50 10.26 N 3 43.38 W
3	072	67.7	074	10:26	14:15	50 31.70 N 02 02.75 W
4	055	4.8	064	1:10	15:26	50 34.46 N 01 56.52 W
5	025	3.9	034	0:48	16:14	50 37.97 N 01 54.00 W
6	331	2.6	333	0:25	16:39	50 40.24 N 01 56.02 W

Passage plan

TIDAL ATLAS PORT　　HW time　　　HW ht　　　Date

-6 -5 -4 -3 -2 -1 HW +1 +2 +3 +4 +5 +6

LOCAL PORT　　Atlas page change over times
　　　　　HW time　　　HW ht　　　LW ht

-6 -5 -4 -3 -2 -1 HW +1 +2 +3 +4 +5 +6

Atlas page change over times

Sp. Range　　　Today's Range　　　Np. Range

Tidal atlas times

I'd be plotting every half hour, but see below for the method. I check the distance run between each fix and compare this with the distance logged and the tidal flow to make sure it makes sense. If the logged distance is 6.5 miles and the tide is running at one knot with us, I would expect the two fixes to be about 7.5 miles apart.

At displacement boat speeds, it pays to plan to steer one continuous heading allowing for the tide along the complete leg, to use the tide to best advantage (see Appendix D). Seapro draws the planned track over the seabed for me so that I can monitor our progress. I show how to do this manually in Appendix D. Provided that we are keeping reasonably close to our planned ground track with no large errors induced by tide and speed different from planned or compass error, I don't alter heading until the halfway point, provided that it's safe to do so. At that stage, I alter heading to get me back on track at the next waypoint. I do this again at

Time BST	Course Steered (C)	Log Dist since	Estimated Course Steered	Estimated Dist Run	Leeway	Wind	Sea	Weather	Vis	Baro	Position	Source of fix	Next WP	Remarks
Date 16 Jun 2007				From SALCOMBE								TO POOLE	AT POOLE	
03:00											Salcombe			Slipped moring - Pilotage to Prawle Point ETA Poole entrance 16:40
13:45	075	4.8				W4	3'	F	Good	1022	WP 2 2ml S Prawle point	QFS	3	Set course 076 M ETA WP 3 14:15
14:45	075	10.8	075	6.0	0	NW4	3'	F	Good	1022	50 12.0 N 03 39.16 W	QFS	3	Autopilot holding heading well
15:45	075	17.1	075	6.3	0	NW4	3'	F	Good	1023	50 14.33 N 03 29.81 W	QFS	3	Start Pt Light 262M Good compass check
16:45	075	23.6	075	6.5	0	N4	3'	F	Mod	1023	50 17.58 N 03 14.24 W	QFS	3	Tide setting us North as expected
17:45	075	30.2	075	6.6	0	N4	3'	F	Poor	1023	50 20.44 N 03 04.16 W	QFS	3	Fog patches - sea temp 14.3C Radar on
18:45	075	36.7	075	6.5	0	N4	3'	F	Mod	1023	50 24.32 N 02 54.71 W	QFS	3	About a knot of tide with us, expect to be out south now ETA WP 3 at 14:30
19:45	075	43.3	075	6.6	0	NW4	3'	F	Good	1024	50 25.44 N 02 43.1 W	QFS	3	Starting to close track, ease out swing now
20:45	075	49.4	075	6.1	0	NW4	3'	F	Good	1024	50 26.33 N 02 32.43 W	QFS	3	Portland Light 042M
21:45	075	55.9	075	6.5	0	N4	3'	F	Good	1024	50 27.12 N 02 24.96 W	QFS	3	Portland light 347M ETA WP 3 14:45, Tide running stronger than expected
22:45	070	64.5	070	6.6	5	NE4	3'	F	Good	1024	50 28.07 N 02 17.63 W	QFS	3	Portland light 300M
23:45	070	71.2	070	6.7	5	NE4	3'	F	Good	1025	50 29.55 N 02 10.85 W	QFS	3	ETA WP3 14:45 ETA Poole ent 17:10
14:45	075	77.8	075	6.6	0	NW4	3'	F	Good	1025	Way point 3	QFS	4	Alter course 060C for WP4
15:00	065	84.0	065	6.2	0	NW4	3'	F	Good	1024	Way point 4	QFS	5	Alter course 035C for WP 5
16:00	065	90.3	065	6.3	0	NW4	3'	F	Good	1024	Way point 5	QFS	6	Alter course 335C for WP 6 - Poole ent
17:15	335	98.3	335	6.0	0	NW4	3'	F	Good	1024	Poole Entrance	Vis		Sails down and motored in last leg - Super sail
17:45		101.2									Off Pottery Pan			At anchor in 3.4 metres

Passage log

half the remaining distance, repeating this every time I halve the distance. As you can see, on this passage, I altered heading only when we started to make leeway as the wind headed us. Although we got 3 miles north of the direct track, we stayed pretty well on our planned ground track.

If you are in a sailing boat, tacking against the wind, tack so that you stay either side of the planned ground track. On an open water passage such as this, it saves navigation effort if you tack on each hourly fix until you get closer to your destination, provided that it's safe to do so and the wind doesn't change direction unfavourably. See Appendix A for the procedure.

Planned ground track

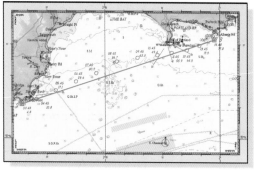

Passage plot

Alternative to Plotting Latitude and Longitude

Plotting latitude and longitude on a small boat at sea is not everyone's 'cup of tea'. There are alternative methods that require more chart work before you start, but simplify the navigator's work on passage. These alternative methods are the only way that you can do any form of chart work on a fast moving boat because of its motion. On a fast motorboat, or any boat in rough seas, thorough planning for all eventualities is a must, as you may not be able to do the paper work on the way.

Note

Some of these methods involve entering coordinates into your GPS which don't form part of a route, so you have no method of cross-checking their accuracy. Do double-check their coordinates and try to check their bearing and direction from a known point, before you use them.

Passage Grid

The passage from Salcombe to Poole, outlined above, could have been made using a passage grid. The GPS set will give the distance to the next waypoint and the cross-track error, provided that the route is active. Using the grid, you can plot your fix by eye using the cross-track error and distance to go. This method is very quick and as accurate as you require.

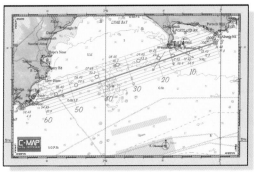

Passage grid

Approach 'Spider's Web'

If you are approaching your destination, you can use an approach spider's web. The closer you get to your destination, the more accurate it is, which is just what you need. This method uses the bearing and distance to your waypoint – just ensure that the GPS bearing and the grid use the same units, either magnetic or true.

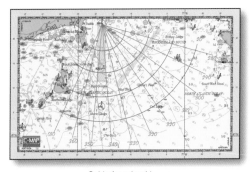

Spider's web grid

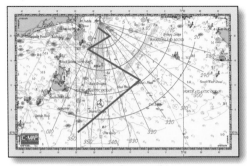

Tacking towards a waypoint

The spider's web is also very good if you are tacking towards your destination, giving shorter tacks as you get nearer.

Compass Rose as a Waypoint

You can avoid a lot of chart preparation by inserting a compass rose as one of your waypoints. You don't actually intend going to it, so you mustn't attempt to navigate towards it. The GPS gives bearing and distance to an active waypoint, so all you need to do is place a position line through the centre of the waypoint (in this case the compass rose), aligning it with the 'far side' as it's a direction towards, and then mark off the distance along the position line from the centre of the compass rose. You now have your fix – again pretty quick and accurate, as long as you use the correct direction, either true or magnetic for both the GPS and the compass rose.

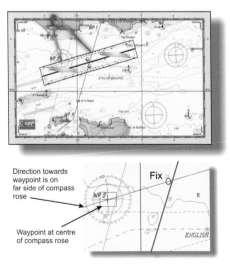

Waypoint at centre of Compass Rose

Unmarked Danger as a Waypoint

If you are worried about going too close to an unmarked danger, such as a dangerous rock, you can put a waypoint at the danger itself. Your GPS will then give you the distance and bearing to the danger so that it can be safely avoided.

 GPS gives distance and bearing (1.36 miles, 320 degrees) to unmarked dangerous rock. 'Pierre au Vraic' allowing it to be safely avoided.

Waypoint at unmarked danger

Clearing Bearing

Another way of avoiding an unmarked danger is to use a clearing bearing. In this case I have drawn a line from the next waypoint (which is now active) towards the danger but giving a safe distance off. This is known as a clearing bearing and in this instance is 030 degrees. Provided that we don't allow the boat to stray too far to the west so that the bearing to the waypoint doesn't exceed 030 degrees, we will be safe. Again, make sure that both the bearing and the GPS are given in either magnetic or true.

Clearing bearing

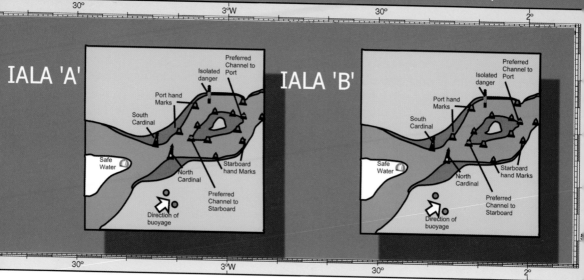

Pilotage

Who Does the Piloting?

Means of Pilotage

International System of Buoyage

Planning

The Basics of Preparing a Pilot Plan

Making a Pilotage Plan

Working as a Team

Whereas *navigation* implies that you are fixing your position by plotting on a chart, *pilotage* means that you are controlling your boat so that it follows a prescribed safe path by visual means. This doesn't mean that you can't use electronic aids, but as we have seen, these can sometimes be highly inaccurate, and often pilotage requires us to position our boat accurately to within 10 to 20 metres.

Pilotage occurs at each end of a passage, so pilotage plans need to be included in your passage planning.

The basic aids to pilotage are the human eye, the hand-bearing compass and a properly calibrated depth sounder, speed log, steering compass and a plan. Electronic aids can add to your armoury.

Who Does the Piloting?

Ideally, the pilot should not have any other duties. You often see the skipper of a leisure boat helming and piloting as well. This isn't desirable. If you haven't sufficient crew, use the autopilot if you have one when pilotage is demanding.

Means of Pilotage

Day or Night?

It would seem obvious that night is different from day! However, there is a fundamental difference that becomes apparent only when you are looking for a lighthouse or lit navigation aid. A flashing light is visible only when the light is 'on'. As the majority of marine lights have a short flash and a long period of darkness, it's likely the light will be visible for only about 10% of the time – for 90% of the time it will be invisible!

Unlit aids to navigation will not be visible at all, so only lit transits are of any use at night. Whereas busy commercial ports lend themselves to easy pilotage at night, estuaries and havens used mostly by leisure sailors may be difficult or impossible to enter at night.

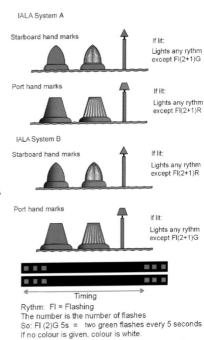

IALA lateral buoyage

International System of Buoyage

The International Association of Lighthouse Authorities (IALA) has standardised the system of buoyage used internationally. Owing to a small disagreement, there are two systems as follows:

IALA System A (IALA-A), used throughout most of the world;

IALA System B (IALA-B), used in the United States of America and those countries which have a close association with the United States of America.

The difference is the colour of the lateral buoys – those marking the edges of a channel:

IALA System A has the *green* buoys on the starboard (right hand) side of the channel when entering a port, whereas IALA System B has the *red* buoys on the starboard side of the channel when entering a port. For those used to IALA System A, remembering the rhyme 'Red Right Returning' when in IALA System B waters is useful.

Where a channel splits into two, both navigable, but where it is preferable to use one, a preferred channel buoy is used. The main body of the buoy is coloured as if it were in the preferred channel, whilst the colour of the band tells you which way to turn.

The chart will show the 'general direction of buoyage' where there is any doubt.

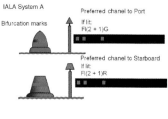
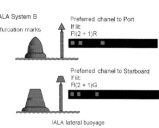

IALA lateral buoyage

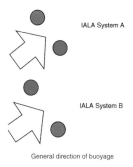

General direction of buoyage

It's essential for the pilot to understand that when proceeding in the direction of buoyage, the starboard hand buoys are passed on the starboard side of the boat, that is leave the green buoys to starboard for IALA-A and leave the red buoys to starboard for IALA-B. When proceeding in the opposite direction, the red buoys are left to starboard (IALA-A) and the green buoys are left to starboard (IALA-B).

Aground, the wrong side of the marker

This applies to the preferred channel marks as well. This means that when travelling in the opposite direction, the preferred channel to starboard buoy means 'turn left'.

Some people find this concept difficult. Having pulled a boat off a mud bank when the skipper had tried to pass a channel buoy on the wrong side, he continued down river still trying to pass the buoys on the incorrect side. He obviously found it difficult to comprehend the reversal of the colours.

International Buoyage – All Areas

The rest of the international system of buoyage is the same in all areas.

Cardinal Buoyage System

This consists of four different buoys that may be placed to the North, East, South or West of a danger. They have differing top-marks, colours and light sequences.

North Cardinal
safe water to
the NORTH of
the hazard

West Cardinal
safe water to
the WEST of
the hazard

East Cardinal
safe water to
the EAST of
the hazard

Hazard

South Cardinal
safe water to
the SOUTH of
the hazard

Cardinal buoyage system IALA "A" & "B"

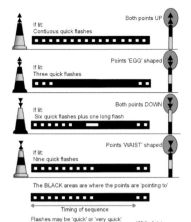

If lit:
Contiuous quick flashes

Both points UP

If lit:
Three quick flashes

Points 'EGG' shaped

If lit:
Six quick flashes plus one long flash

Both points DOWN

If lit:
Nine quick flashes

Points 'WAIST' shaped

The BLACK areas are where the points are 'pointing to'

Timing of sequence

Flashes may be 'quick' or 'very quick'
(60 or 90 flashes per second)
Timing may be 5, 10 or 15 seconds

White light

Cardinal buoyage system IALA "A" & "B"

In order to use the cardinal system reference must be made to a compass.

Safe Water Mark

Indicates 'safe water' and often used at the start of a channel as an 'aiming point'.

Top mark, if fitted, RED ball

If lit:
Iso, or   White light
Oc, or
LFl.10s or
Mo(A)
What this means is much more light than is usual for a buoy

IALA safe water mark (the fairway buoy)

Isolated Danger Mark

Placed on, or very close to, an isolated danger. Don't get too close to these as the danger may extend well from the mark, so have a look at the chart. This is the only buoy with a light characteristic of 'flashing 2 white'

Top mark – Two BLACK balls

If lit: White light

This is the only Fl(2) anywhere
If you see this - keep clear

IALA isolated danger mark

Special Mark

These are non-navigational in nature and are used as yacht racing marks, to show the boundaries of danger areas and to indicate water skiing areas etc.

If lit, the lights are yellow

Top mark, if fitted, a yellow cross
If lit:
Fl. Y   Yellow light

IALA 'Special' marks

Emergency Wreck Marking Buoy

Introduce in 2007, these buoys can be quickly placed around a new wreck prior to normal buoys being laid if required. Where several buoys are used to mark the same wreck, the flashing lights are synchronised.

These diagrams show how the IALA buoys may be used.

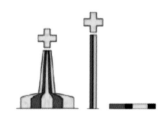

Emergency wreck-marking buoy

Narrow Channel Marked by Buoys or Beacons at Frequent Intervals

This is the easiest form of pilotage; just keep in the channel. At night, it's desirable to have a list of directions and distances between each buoy.

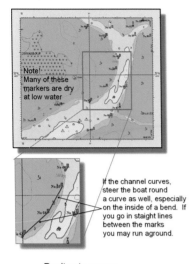

Note!
Many of these markers are dry at low water

If the channel curves, steer the boat round a curve as well, especially on the inside of a bend. If you go in staight lines between the marks you may run aground.

Don't cut corners

Narrow channel, IALA B, with depths in feet and NOAA chart symbols.

Just follow the buoys

In a curved channel, the channel will curve between individual buoys or beacons, so if you follow a straight line between buoys, you may run into shallows, which curve between them. You need to allow for this curvature.

In a very narrow channel, the buoys, or especially any beacons, may be in water too shallow for your boat at low water, so don't get too close to them. You have to balance this with the requirement to keep as far to the starboard of the channel as safely possible (Colregs Rule 9a)

Channel Marked by Buoys or Beacons Some Distance Apart

In this type of channel, you definitely need to have a list of directions and distances between buoys. At night or in poor visibility, you may depart one buoy and may not see the next for some time. You can easily lose your sense of direction, especially if there's a cross-tide, so use the hand-bearing compass when looking for the next buoy.

The reason for the marker is obvious
The channel markers are there for a purpose

Channels Marked by Transits

As outlined in Chapter 8, transits are the most accurate form of position line. Harbour authorities often install transits, lit or unlit, to mark the centreline of their channels. If you

Transits
open

Transits
closing

Transits
in line

Using a transit

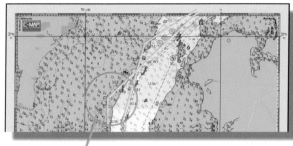

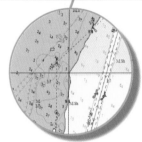

Multiple lit transits in the
shallow Chesapeake bay
allow accurate alignment
in the channels without
recourse to too many
buoys.

Transits lit by high intensity
directional lights

haven't used a particular transit before, check the bearing to make sure it's the correct one and remember that the charted bearing is in degrees true.

Transits designed specifically for ships with high bridges may give false information to leisure craft. At Hamble BP Oil terminal there are transits to guide the tankers onto the berth. Although the back transit is higher than the front, as it should be, from the cockpit of a small boat the front appears higher, so you could easily turn in the wrong direction to keep the lights in line!

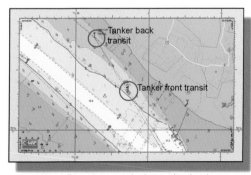

Very tall transit towers give impression that the
front light is higher than the back light from the
cockpit of a small boat

Tall transit towers

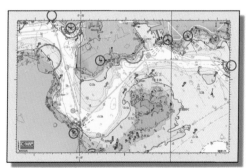

A series of seven tightly sectored red, green and white
lights guide the pilot into Devonport Harbour, reducing
the number of channel markers required in the
deep-water channel.

Sectored lights

In place of transits some channels are marked by sectored lights, some to avoid dangers outside the channel and some so narrow and directionally accurate that you can use them to stay in the correct side of the channel!

No Formal Aids to Pilotage

If there's no charted marks, transits, etc., then you have to make up your own. You have basically four choices:

- Try and find charted features that can be aligned to give a safe transit. With natural transits you need to be aware that buildings may have been demolished or had something built in front of them. Even natural transits in pilot books may have been painted in a different colour, trees may have grown or been chopped down. You always need a fallback.

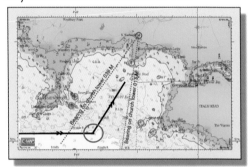

- Mark bearings on your chart from easily visible landmarks, natural or man-made, and use a hand-bearing compass to stay on the bearing.

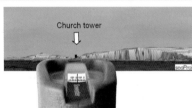

Initial approach to river Yealm

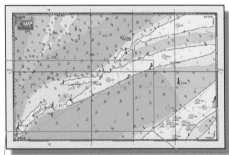

It will be difficult to find your way along this channel in poor visibility or at night, so note the directions and distances

074M
0.75NM

059M
1.2NM

070M
1.95NM

092M
0.53NM

Channel with few buoys

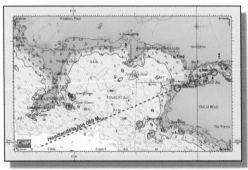

A natural transit of the two headlands in line on 069 degrees magnetic. In case you can't define the actual headlands, you'll need a fallback plan.

A natural transit

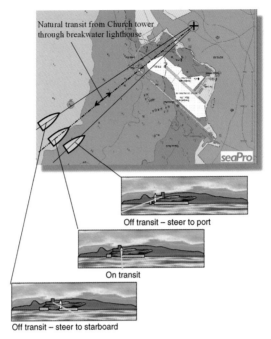

Natural transit from Church tower
through breakwater lighthouse

Off transit – steer to port

On transit

Off transit – steer to starboard

Choosing your own 'natural' transit

- Mark bearings on your chart that will keep you clear of hazards. These are known as clearing bearings.
- Use your calibrated depth sounder to follow depth contours.

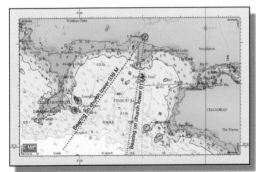

If you approach from outside the 20 metres depth contour keeping the bearing of the church tower not more than 039 degrees M and not less than 013 degrees M you will have a safe passage, provided you don't go north of the inbound transit into the River Yealm

Clearing bearings

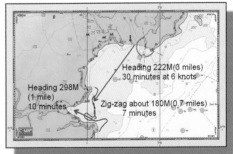

Heading 222M(3 miles)
30 minutes at 6 knots

Heading 298M
(1 mile)
10 minutes

Zig-zag about 180M(0.7 miles)
7 minutes

To find the entrance to Helford river from Falmouth in misty conditions, you could make a course to the north of the entrance turning South when you get to the 5 metres contour as indicated by your calibrated depth sounder.
Zig-zag along the contour until you get to deep channel and then turn onto the inbound heading.

Using a depth contour

Planning

Pilotage requires planning. If you've been there before, the plan may be in your head, but it has been planned. Your old plan will need to be updated for the weather and tide on the day.

Just like passage planning, of which this becomes part, start off with an overview and assemble the tools you will need, such as large- and small-scale charts, almanac and pilotage notes.

The Basics of Preparing a Pilot Plan

- Pilotage is visual navigation
- Pilotage needs to be planned
- Use large-scale charts
- Check dangers
- Check special rules
- Check VHF channels

Aids to Pilotage:

- Pilot book
- Tidal atlas
- A pilotage plan
- Hand-bearing compass
- Binoculars
- Log distance
- Depth
- GPS – course over ground
- Stop watch
- Radar

Methods:

- Clearing bearings
- Charted transits
- Natural transits

- Sailing along contours
- Course to steer
- Distance/time run
- Recognition of buoys/lights
- Pilot 'pilots' – helmsman steers

Making a Pilotage Plan

To make this exercise more realistic, we'll make a pilotage plan from Plymouth breakwater to the river Yealm on 1st August 2007. In making the plan, you will also be 'rehearsing' how you will conduct the passage.

- Firstly, put the general route onto the chart. Choose a scale so that you can get the complete passage on one chart and then measure distances and bearings. I list the bearings in degrees magnetic as all my direction instruments at the helm also use degrees magnetic.

- Now, if necessary on a smaller scale chart, look at how you can pilot the first leg. At Duke Rock east cardinal buoy you can check your depth sounder, which should read 6 metres plus the rise of tide. The compass can be checked for gross error as you head for

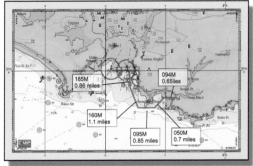

Overview of pilotage plan from Plymouth breakwater to river Yealm

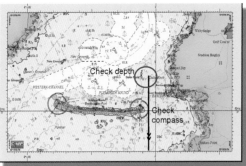

Plymouth breakwater

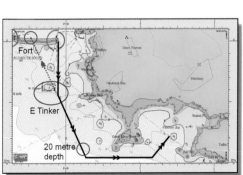

Pilotage for first part of passage

the eastern end of the breakwater, as there should be little cross-tide here. If you have GPS, the COG should be monitored at all times to help ensure that you are achieving the desired tracks.

- Continue on this heading until you reach the East Tinker cardinal buoy. Maintain the heading of 185M until you see the East Tinker cardinal behind you aligned with the Breakwater fort. Now turn onto 160 magnetic and adjust heading to keep the East Tinker in transit with the Breakwater fort (back bearing of 340M) until you reach the 20-metre depth contour. Continue for 0.15 mile (1.5 minutes at 6 knots) and then turn onto 095M.

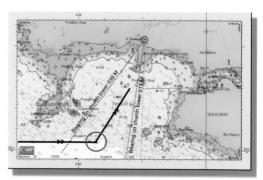

- Continue eastwards to make good a ground track of 095M, allowing for any tide. Your GPS, set to display COG will help to ensure you keep on track. Ensure that the depth remains at 20 metres or more so that you keep well clear of the drying rock to the south of the Great Mew Stone. As you clear the Great Mew Stone, start looking for the church tower. Looking on about 055M with your hand-held compass will help you find it. You can start your approach to the Yealm once the bearing of the church tower is 039M or less. Ensure that the bearing does not reduce below 019M in order to avoid all obstacles.

Initial approach to river Yealm

- Now start looking eastwards watching for Misery Point to become visible beyond Mouthstone Point. You should soon see the transit beacons well up the wooded slope above Cellar Bay. Once these are in transit turn onto 093M and keep them lined up.

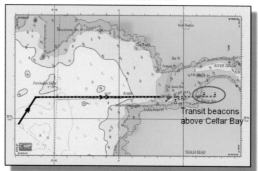

Transit into Yealm entrance

- As you approach the two red buoys (April–October) you will have to 'jiggle' south and leave them to port. Start looking for a red and white marker post high on the north bank. If you steer to keep that on a bearing of 050M, you'll keep in the deepest water while crossing the inner bar.

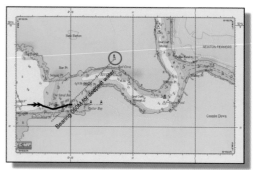

Entering the Yealm, avoiding the bar

- You are now in the river, but your plan doesn't end until you are where you intend to moor. I've had many students, who having entered the harbour have no idea which way to go or even what they are looking for!

- Some harbours (though not the Yealm) have a Port Signal Station that shows a series of 'traffic' lights controlling your progress. Ensure you know what these lights mean.

The river Yealm

The Paper Plan to Use in the Cockpit

There are a number of methods of writing your notes. What is essential is that pilotage is done from the cockpit. This is not the time when you want to be at the chart table. Your notes need to be simple, concise and clear.

- If you are good at sketching, draw a sketch map with all the details on it.
- The other method is a 'strip' plan.

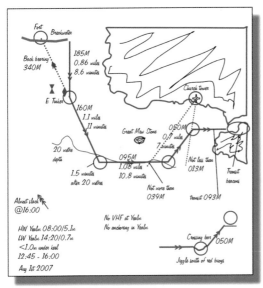

Sketch pilot plan

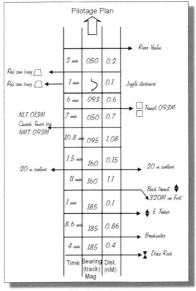

Strip pilotage plan

- The problem with using a 'proper' chart is that there's just too much detail, although you can put one inside a transparent chart folder and use a wax pencil to draw on the plastic. This also keeps the chart dry and prevents it blowing overboard.

Working as a Team

The pilot needs to ensure that the helmsman understands what is intended, so brief him properly. If you are both pilot and helmsman, use the autopilot if you have one. When in pilotage waters in a sailing boat, consider motoring instead of sailing, especially if you are short handed and in unfamiliar waters.

Initial transit alignment

The buoy has moved to starboard - turn to starboard

- If the next course is towards a buoy or marker, make sure that it's identified properly. Pointing in its general direction won't do, especially as you will be looking at it from a different perspective. Note a feature on the horizon, say a tree, and relate the position of the buoy with the tree – 'It's three hand width's to the left of that tree sticking above all the others'. If there's no feature, stand behind the helmsman and point to it with your outstretched arm over his shoulder, to give the same perspective.

The buoy has moved to port - turn to port

Keep the buoy aligned with something in the background

- At night, this is even more important, as most of the time the buoy will be invisible! Firstly, the pilot needs to identify it himself. Before you get to the end of this leg, use the hand-bearing compass on the expected bearing to find the light defining the next leg and then identify its light sequence. Now point over the helmsman's shoulder towards the buoy and as the light flashes 'announce' each flash 'Flash-Flash-Flash' in time with the light. This will ensure that the helmsman is 'seeing' the same light as you are.
- If there's a cross-tide, asking the helmsman to 'steer for that buoy' is a recipe for disaster. Tell the helmsman which way the tide is flowing. If it's from port to starboard, tell him that he needs to aim 'off to port' and 'keep the buoy on the starboard bow'. If there's an object on the horizon above the buoy – that tree again – tell him to keep the tree and the buoy in transit and explain what you mean if necessary. 'If the buoy moves to port, you must steer to port to bring them back into line' and vice-versa. If there's nothing to use as a transit, ahead or astern, give him a course to steer allowing for the tide, or use the GPS COG as an aid.
- At night, if you're on a transit, help the helmsman, as he will be steering a course.

- If you're on a 'back transit', that is the transit is behind you, remember that the course corrections are the same – if the nearer object moves to port, then you steer to port. Don't use the terms left and right as these are reversed when you look behind you.

- If you are keeping on a bearing to an object, or a clearing bearing, the helmsman should be given a course to steer. You should monitor the bearing as often as necessary and give the helmsman course corrections 'come 5 degrees port onto 045'.

- Once you know that the helmsman is established on the current leg of the passage, monitor him loosely, but start looking for the next object. If you're looking for an object – a tower, say– then identify it in good time, using your hand-bearing compass and binoculars if necessary.

- If you can't find the next object, check your time and distance run since the last. Don't run blindly on into dangerous waters in the hope of seeing it. Either the tide is a lot different to what you assumed or you have made an error in measuring the distance or bearing. On many occasions when teaching pilotage, the lost

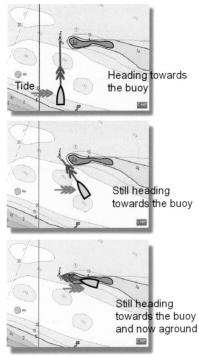

Heading towards the buoy

Still heading towards the buoy

Still heading towards the buoy and now aground

Just keep heading towards the buoy

buoy is just off to one side, but the student navigator has been concentrating on just looking ahead. If the helmsman or other crew members are all 'in the picture' they are likely to have spotted it.

Automatic Identification System

What is Automatic Identification System?

Automatic identification system (AIS) allows a transmitter on a ship to broadcast information about the course, speed and position, etc. (dynamic data – navigation information) and also destination, type, MMSI and name, etc. (static information) of the vessel. Receivers on other ships and shore stations can display this information as an aid to collision avoidance, traffic control or national security. The system is compulsory for vessels of 300 tonnes or more and the experience gained over the last couple of years has been very positive, although there are problems that are discussed below.

How Does AIS Work?

Each minute of time is divided into 2250 discrete 'time stamped' slots in each of two VHF, line of sight 'channels'. A set will listen for other transmissions to find a vacant slot and then 'reserves' this slot for its own regular transmissions. If all the slots are busy, it looks for a much weaker signal (indicating a greater range) and takes this slot. This is known as 'self-organising'. In very busy areas, the range at which contacts can be seen slowly deteriorates.

Class A AIS

This is the compulsory system fitted by commercial shipping worldwide. It transmits a great deal of data, much of which, such as destination etc., is entered manually by the bridge crew and the rest, such as GPS position, is wired directly from the ship's equipment. The heading information from the compass system has often been found unreliable, as has the data that has been manually entered.

The dynamic information is updated every 10 seconds for vessels up to 14 knots and every 2 seconds for vessels travelling at more than 23 knots and the transmitting power is 12.5 watts.

Class B AIS

This is a simpler and cheaper system designed for 'voluntary fit' vessels and transmits at only 1 or 2 watts. It has a built-in GPS and the 'dynamic' data consists of only position, COG and SOG, although heading may be added. Data is transmitted at only 30-second intervals and the set cannot reserve slots ahead. Instead, it has to listen for an unused slot, or a slot with

a much weaker signal, on 10 randomly selected slots over a 10-second period. If no slot is available, it cannot transmit and must wait a further 30 seconds and try again. A class B set may thus not be able to transmit regularly even when there are many empty slots as the randomly selected slots may be full.

AIS Displays

On the leisure market there are two types of display available. Ideally the AIS receiver is connected to a chartplotter (or pc plotter) and the 'target' information is displayed in the form of a 'ship icon' together with its course and speed and whether it is a danger. You can see all the other data if required. All targets in range will be displayed on the screen in a dynamic way. The other alternative is to have a dedicated display, such as that from NASA, where up to 30 targets are shown on a circular 'plan position indicator' (PPI) although no indication of your own course is shown on the north-up display.

Most merchant ships have a far less sophisticated navigation display than many leisure craft. Only the very newly built ships have large colour radar screens, electronic chart displays and few have the AIS information co-located on the radar or chartplotter. Most show their AIS data on a very simplified display. This is required to display the data of only three vessels at any one time, showing the distance bearing and name of the vessels although many do have the ability to show more or have a simple PPI. Often, because of the limitations of older bridge design, the AIS data is not within easy view of the Officer of the Watch.

Cursor
Distance and bearing of the cursor from your boat

Your boat   AIS targets

AIS display on chartplotter

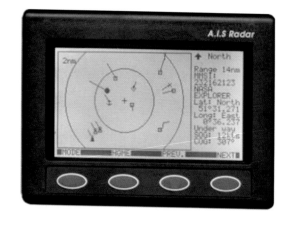

All new builds from July 2008 will have to have an integrated AIS display, but this will not be retrospective.

The AIS Display on a Chartplotter

When the chartplotter is supplied with data from an AIS receiver, all AIS equipped ships within range will be displayed on the chartplotter screen. These ships will be shown as a triangle with a line projected in front of it representing the ship's COG. If you 'hover' the screen's cursor over the triangle, more information will be displayed, consisting of at least

When the cursor is 'hovered' over target, a 'pop-up' box will appear. The target is 2.839 miles from us and the CPA is only 0.64 mile, which is uncomfortably close with all the 'sea-room' available.

AIS target information box

- the name of the ship,
- the ship's MMSI,
- the ship's international call-sign,
- the ship's COG,
- the ship's SOG,
- the CPA (closest point of approach),
- the TCPA (time to CPA).

The distance and bearing of the cursor from your boat will be given on the screen so if the cursor is on the target ship you will have its range and bearing.

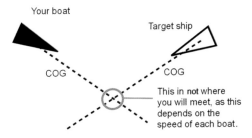

Your boat

Target ship

COG   COG

This in not where you will meet, as this depends on the speed of each boat.

What the Display Tells You

Looking at the basic chartplotter display, it's difficult to know if any target will pass ahead, collide or pass astern of you. You could resolve the situation graphically, but the AIS computer will do the sums for you. If the transmission from the target contains errors, then a false CPA and TCPA may be displayed.

As far as collision avoidance is concerned, the important information is CPA and TCPA, displayed in the AIS information box. From this you can judge what action, if any, you should take. It's worth stating here that your actions are dictated by the International Regulations for Prevention of Collisions at Sea (Colregs).

With only this information the target could pass ahead, collide with you or pass astern.

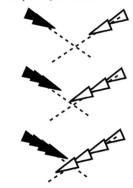

In this instance, the faster ship will pass ahead of you.

Basic AIS display

The action to be taken differs if you can or can't see the target visually, but as the rules were written long before AIS was conceived, it's unclear if rule 19 applies to vessels seen only by `AIS' rather than `only by radar'.

Normally, you can enter a value of CPA at which you would be uncomfortable. If a target is predicted to get this close (or closer) to you, the triangle will blink on and off and you'll get an audible alarm.

A receiver-only AIS on *your* boat will allow you to monitor commercial shipping as an aid to making collision avoidance decisions. Because of some unreliability of data, especially heading, it must not be taken as an absolute indication of the situation, but in conjunction with radar, it is an exceptionally good situational awareness tool.

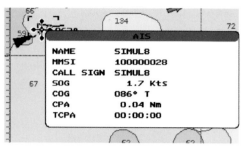

The AIS information box

Saga Rose is at anchor, but AIS indicates that she is under way using engine

Whitstar, which has just refuelled Saga Rose, is under way using engine, but her AIS indicates that she is still moored.

Erroneous AIS indications

Advantages of AIS

- It can see around corners, such as headlands or bends, unlike radar, which can't.

- It can give you the name and MMSI of a ship which you may wish to call.

- It can give you the closest point of approach of the target vessel.

Disadvantages of AIS

- Only commercial vessels bigger than 300 GRT are required to fit it – you can see only vessels which have it fitted.

- It can transmit erroneous information.

AIS Class B Transceiver

If we fit a class B AIS transceiver (transmitter/receiver) we must be aware of its limitations:

- There is absolutely no guarantee that any commercial vessel will see our class B transmissions, either because of lack of output power, because our set cannot find a free slot or because of deficiencies of their AIS display. Even if they can 'see' us, with only 30-second updating at best, our intentions may not be clear.

- A recent paper by Andy Norris in the Journal of Navigation published by the Royal Institute of Navigation summed it up thus: *Any confidence that the potential user of class B equipment has in expecting own-vessel's presence to be highlighted to all surrounding SOLAS vessels is misplaced.*

- If we wish to maximise the chances of our vessel being seen by commercial vessels, our best chance is to ensure that our boat will appear on their radar screen. The best way of achieving this is probably to fit an 'active' radar reflector, such as See Me, rather than rely on many of the so-called radar reflectors currently on the market. Some, commonly seen, have such poor radar reflectivity as to be almost useless.

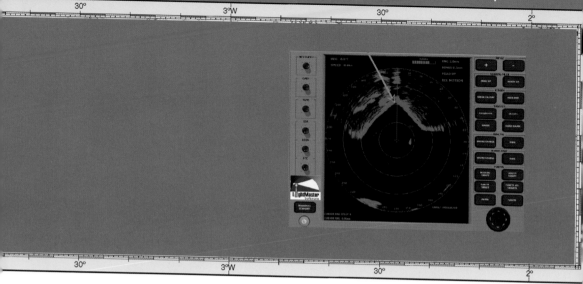

Radar

How Radar Works

Navigation Using Radar

Pilotage Using Radar

Radar Overlay on a Chart Plotter

Setting up Your Radar

Radar Used for Collision Avoidance

The majority of boat owners buy radar for collision avoidance, for which proper training is required. However, radar is a very powerful navigation and pilotage tool as well.

How Radar Works

The radar scanner rotates at approximately 24 revolutions per minute, and while it does this, it transmits pulses of microwave energy. The time interval between each pulse is long enough to allow a pulse to travel out to the maximum range of the radar and back to the scanner. This means that the radar is listening for about 99.9% of the time and transmitting for less than 0.1%. Although each pulse may be 2 or 4 kilowatts, the average power is only 2 to 4 watts.

Measuring Range

If one of these pulses strikes a solid object the pulse is reflected back to the scanner and the time taken for the return journey is used to calculate the distance of the target from your boat.

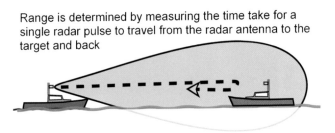

Range is determined by measuring the time take for a single radar pulse to travel from the radar antenna to the target and back

Measuring range

Measuring Bearing

At the time a returning 'echo' is received, the radar measures the angle of the scanner from the bows of the boat. Because the pulse travels at the speed of light, this is effectively the bearing of the target from the bows. The radar knows nothing about compass

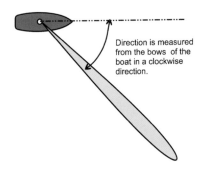

Direction is measured from the bows of the boat in a clockwise direction.

Measuring of direction

direction, so unless it is supplied with direction from an external electronic 'fluxgate' compass or a GPS, it can give direction only in degrees 'relative'. If a GPS heading input is used, radar can measure magnetic direction only when the boat is moving.

The Reflectivity of a 'Target'

The reflectivity of the target depends on its angle to the radar beam, its size, its surface texture and what it's made of. The diagrams here give some idea of how the angle and the texture affect how much signal is returned to the radar scanner.

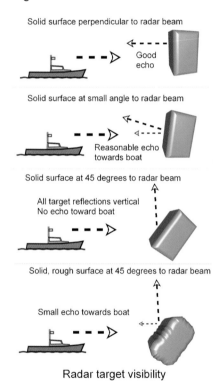

Solid surface perpendicular to radar beam

Good echo

Solid surface at small angle to radar beam

Reasonable echo towards boat

Solid surface at 45 degrees to radar beam

All target reflections vertical
No echo toward boat

Solid, rough surface at 45 degrees to radar beam

Small echo towards boat

Radar target visibility

The Size of the Pulse

A long pulse contains more energy than a short one and so can travel farther to a target and return to the scanner before the pulse is too small to be detected by the radar set.

Two targets close enough together so that they are 'illuminated' by the pulse at the same time will show

Range setting	Pulse length (micro seconds)	Pulse length (metres)
0.75 mile or less	0.08	24
Above 0.75 mile and less than 6.0 mile	0.25	75
6 miles or greater	0.70	210

Typical radar pulse lengths
(Raytheon SL 70 radar)

up on the radar screen as only one target. Ideally then, the pulse should be as short as possible, exactly the opposite to the requirement for the pulse to travel as far as possible.

Professional sets allow the operator to select the pulse length manually, but on a 'leisure' set, the pulse length is controlled by the range selected. Generally, there are about three different pulse lengths, associated with different range scales. The

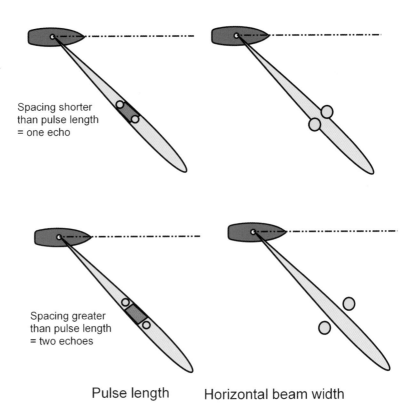

Spacing shorter than pulse length = one echo

Spacing greater than pulse length = two echoes

Pulse length   Horizontal beam width

shortest is about 25 metres in length and the longest about 100 to 125 metres in length. Thus at the lower ranges two buoys 30 metres apart will show as two 'echoes' on the screen, while at the longest range, the targets would need to be 100 metres apart before they showed as two echoes.

Horizontal Beam Width

To distinguish between two targets close together, the beam should be as narrow as possible. Beam width is controlled by the width of the scanner, a smaller scanner having a larger

Entrance to Portsmouth Harbour is invisible at this range

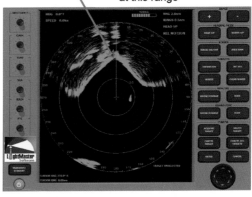

Horizontal beam width of 8 degrees

beam width. Typically, a 12-inch scanner will have a beam 8 degrees wide, while a 24-inch scanner' beam is about 3 degrees wide. The average 18-inch scanner has a horizontal beam width of 5 degrees. Any two targets falling within the width of the beam will show up as only one echo. When navigating, this may mean that a harbour or river entrance may not be visible on the radar screen until you are close enough to allow the beam to pass through the entrance.

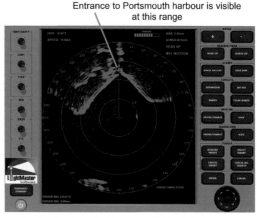

Entrance to Portsmouth harbour is visible at this range

Radar horizontal beam width 2.5 degrees

Vertical Beam Width

A typical vertical beam width is between 25 and 30 degrees wide. This allows the boat to roll from side to side without lifting the radar beam off the surface of the water. A boat has only to roll 12 to 15 degrees before the beam is lifted off the surface, so a sailing boat going to windward may have to de-power to reduce the angle of heel to make the radar useable.

Navigation Using Radar

The 'radar horizon' is slightly farther away than the 'visual horizon' because the beam curves slightly around the Earth's surface. Atmospheric conditions can alter the curvature, so that in high-pressure conditions radar can see farther and in low-pressure situations less far.

Radar power output determines the maximum range, so that distant high points can be seen farther away with a more powerful radar. However, the most important advantage of high power is that the radar can see smaller targets more easily.

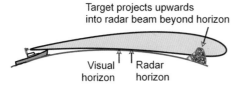

Target projects upwards into radar beam beyond horizon

Visual horizon | Radar horizon

The radar horizon

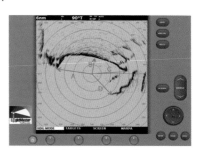

Distance A = 3.8 nautical miles
Distance B = 1.8 nautical miles
Distance C = 3.6 nautical miles
Distance D = 3.25 nautical miles

Navigation by radar ranges

When taking a three-position line fix, one normally tends to think of using bearings. When using radar, bearings are not the tool of choice. Firstly, radar bearings are not very accurate for various reasons; they need to be corrected for deviation and variation, and you need to allow for the horizontal width of the radar beam.

Radar ranges are more accurate, need no correction and are easy to plot, so think 'range first and use bearings only if you have nothing else'.

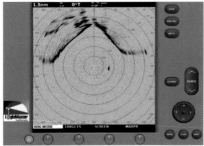

Note: 'B' is parallel to the shore, not a radius.

Navigation fix by radar ranges

You need to be able to recognise suitable points both on the chart and on the radar screen. Don't be tempted into using the 'wrong bay'. Measure the 'width' of the bay on the screen (using the range rings and your fingers) and compare this with the width of the bay on the chart using the chart scale. I've seen students identifying a 4-mile wide bay on the radar as a 1-mile wide bay on the chart!

Whereas range from a point is marked on the chart as a curved position line using a pair of compasses, a distance off a beach, say, is marked by a line parallel to the beach.

A radar fix obtained this way will give you a position relative to the real land, not in terms of latitude and longitude as when using GPS, which may be in error.

Pilotage Using Radar

If you see your destination on radar, don't just 'point and go'. Underwater obstructions and shallows can't be seen by radar, and doing so a recipe for disaster.

Do use 'north-up' display for pilotage. It gets very messy and complicated if you don't, as you will have to keep resetting the electronic bearing lines (EBLs) every time you change heading!

Radar pilotage needs planning, as before, but you have an additional tool, which is distance from an object. Use is made of the radar's EBL and variable range marker (VRM). Most sets have two of

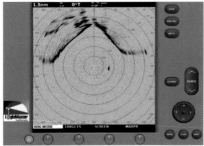

We can see the entrance to Portsmouth Harbour so we just 'point and go'. If we look at the chart we can see that we stand a very good chance of running aground, using this tactic.

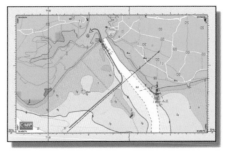

The route we wish to follow into Portsmouth Harbour using the Swashway and the small boat channel that runs just outside and to the south-west of the deep water channel, shown here in red.

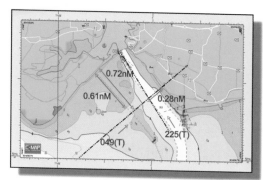

The distances we need to set up the VRMs and the tracks we need to set up the EBLs on the radar display.

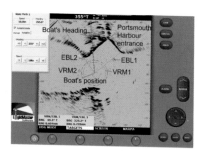

Initial approach.   VRM/EBL1 set to 049.4(T) / 0.604nM
                    VRM/EBL2 set to 325(T) / 0.705nM
Boat's heading 355(T) to close shore to maintain a 'distance off' of 0.6 to 0.71 nautical mile.
The radar is set to display 'north-up' and the range is set at 3 miles and for clarity, the range rings have been switched off.

Initial pilotage approach

Closing shore, now on a heading of 015(T), radar range set at 3 miles.

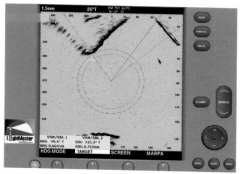

Almost at the correct 'distance off', on a heading of 035(T). Radar range set at 1.5 nautical miles.

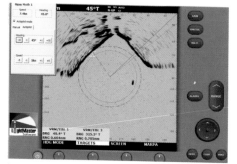

Well established in 'Swashway' at a 'distance off' of about 0.63 nautical miles on a healing of 045 (T) – one VRM 'wheeel' over the shoreline, the other clear.
Radar range still set at 1.5 nautical miles.

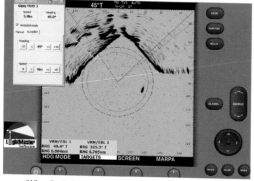

'Wheeling' nicely along the Swashway and watching the depth sounder carefully.

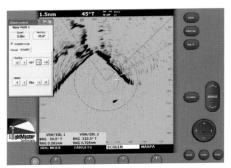

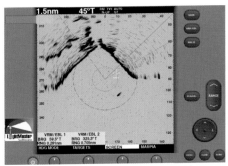

Still maintaining the correct 'distance off'. Approaching the northeastern shore, so resetting VRM1 to 0.28 nM, the 'distance off' that we being our turn onto a heading of 325(T). Still watching the depth carefully.

Just reaching 0.28 mile off the northeastern shore, so starting the turn onto 325(T). The cross-check here is that the depth is now increasing to greater then 5 metres.

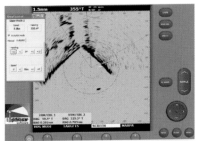

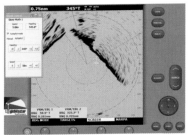

Turned onto a heading of 355(T), EBL2 (325T) is nearly pointing at southern point of entrance, so maintaining heading 355 of 355 for a little longer.

Changed range to 0.75 mile, come port 10 degrees onto a heading 345(T) as EBL2 is now very nearly on the southern point of the entrance. Depth now is between five and ten metres.

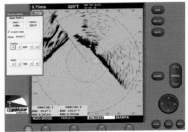

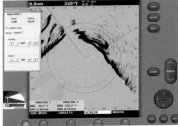

EBL2 now on southern point of entrance and heading 325.

Nicely established in small boat channel. Range set to 0.5 mile.

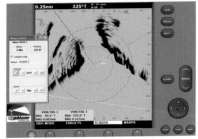

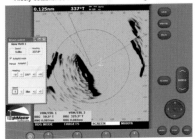

Almost at entrance, range changed to 0.25 mile.

Inside entrance, range set at 0.125 mile and heading 337(T).

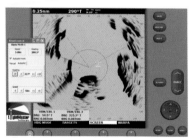

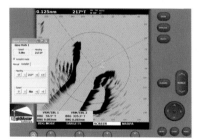

Through entrance, range set at 0.25 mile, heading 290, turning onto a heading of 217(T) to destination.

Now on a heading of 217(T), range set at 0.125 mile, proceeding down channel to destination.

each of these, which can be used to find the direction and bearing of targets. In the case of pilotage, we can pre-set these to help us follow our plan. Professional sets allow what is called 'parallel indexing', an excellent aid to pilotage, but we are able to use VRMs instead and if your radar is able to 'float' your EBL/VRM pair, you have a direct equivalent of parallel indexing.

In order to describe the method of using the radar for pilotage, I have set up an approach to Portsmouth Harbour using Lightmaster Software's radar simulator. Having made our plan, we start our approach from the Solent and aim for the shallow water 'Swashway'. We then maintain the desired distance off the northwestern coast to remain in the channel, turn for the entrance when the distance off the northeastern shore is correct and follow the bearing into the entrance, remaining in the small boat channel, just outside the main, deepwater, channel. In a real situation you will be monitoring the depth sounder as well. The following sequence of diagrams shows the process.

Floating EBL/VRM

Some radar sets allow the VRM/EBL origin to be offset, or floated. This allows pilotage where there's not a long straight piece of land with a good radar echo. Because the floated EBL and VRM are anchored to a static radar target or indeed a static position anywhere on the radar screen, we can define a route to be followed, just as we would follow a visual

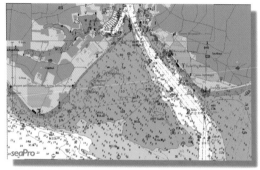

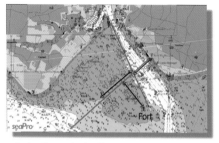

Chart of entrance to Portsmouth

Radar pilotage plan into Portsmouth Harbour entrance using the 'Swashway' and 'small boat channel'.

Pilotage plan details

transit. To do this, the radar must be used in north-up mode. Let us follow the same route into Portsmouth Harbour as before, but this time we'll use the fort and the northeastern shores to guide us in. There are a number of ways that we could set up the radar, but using the radar simulator, we'll follow through a suitable procedure. I've removed all the buoys from the display so that we can just concentrate on the things we are going to use.

- Mark on the approach chart into Portsmouth the centrelines of the Swashway and the small boat channel.
- Measure the direction of the Swashway and the distance off that it passes from the fort. Note also the point before which you want to be established on the centreline.
- Measure the direction of the small boat channel and the distance off the shore that it cuts the Swashway.

VRM/EBL 1 is set to a BRG of 229 T and a RNG of 0.31 mile.
VRM/EBL 2 is set to a BRG of 049 T and a RNG of 0.31 mile.

VRM/EBL 1 is 'floated' so that the bearing passes along the NW side of the fort and the and the VRM is centred on the shoreline
VRM/EBL is floated so that its EBL touches he VRM 1 to become the centreline of the Swashway.

Radar preparation 1

VRM/EBL 1 is now floated to coincide with EBL 2.

This forms the centreline of the Swashway that you are going to use for radar pilotage.

Radar preparation 2

- Set up a VRM/EBL to the reciprocal direction of the Swashway and the distance off from the fort.
- Float this to the coast and place the EBL just touching the NW edge of the fort.

Set up the second EBL/VRM to the direction of the Swashway and the distance off from the fort.

- Float this to a position where the Swashway starts and so that the VRM touches the first EBL.
- Move the first EBL so that it is superimposed on the second. This is the centreline of the Swashway.
- Reset the second (now redundant) EBL/VRM to the direction of the small boat channel and the distance off the north-east shore where you will start to follow it.

VRM/EBL 2 is set to BRG 334 T/0.29 nm.
It is then floated so that the VRM touches the shoreline
and is centred on EBL 1.

This marks the centreline of the small boat channel and
the point at which the change of course is made.

Radar preparation 3

Having constructed the plan on the radar, all you
need to do is to follow it.

The boat is heading 000T and is about 0.25 mile from
the centre line of the Swashway.

Following the plan 1

The boat is now steered to maintain the centreline
of the Swashway – the current heading is 040T.

Following the plan 2

Heading is now 049T and the boat is now approaching the
small boat channel.

Following the plan 3

- Float this EBL/VRM so that the VRM just touches the shore and its centre is on the Swashway centreline.

This probably sounds a bit complicated, but follow the procedure through on the radar simulator screen shots and you will see that it isn't half as complicated as it sounds.

Boat has reached the centreline of the small boat channel and is
turning through 018T onto a heading of 334T

Following the plan 4

The boat is now on the Swashway's centreline and
heading 336T

Following the plan 5

- Approach the Swashway centreline from a safe distance. Here we are approaching on a northerly heading and have about a quarter of a mile to run.

- Turn onto the inbound heading and settle down on the centreline, adjusting the heading as required to allow for wind and tide.

- Keep monitoring the depth throughout the approach.

- As you approach the junction of the two legs, be ready to initiate a turn onto the heading of the small boat channel.

- Now keep on the centreline of the small boat channel.

The boat is well along the small boat channel, on its centreline and heading 334T.

Following the plan 6

Parallel Indexing

Using one 'floated' VRM/EBL, and one normal EBL, the screen can be set up for the equivalent of the professional set's parallel index.

- Set up one VRM/EBL with the course as the bearing and the required 'distance off' VRM.

- Float it sideways so that the floated EBL sits on the target echo.

- Set up the second VRM/EBL with the VRM at the required distance off the target echo.

- Wheel the normal, unfloated, VRM (which remains attached to the boat) along the floated EBL.

- This will allow you to steer the boat along the parallel course, compensating for the tide and wind, passing the target at the required distance off.

Your radar is set up and you're now ready to follow the plan.

Each piloting situation is different so you'll need to consider how the radar can be used. It will depend on how accurately the shoreline or other targets will show up on the screen, cliffs showing up very well while low-lying 'beachy' shorelines may be very indistinct. In some situations radar will be of little use in avoiding underwater dangers, because there's no suitable radar target to line up on.

The floated VRM/EBL is just touching the fort

The normal VRM is set to the same distance and is 'wheeled' along the parallel index formed by the floated EBL

Parallel indexing

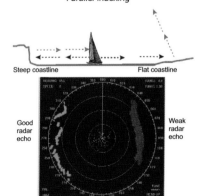

Steep coastline   Flat coastline

Good radar echo   Weak radar echo

Effect of different types of coastline

Radar Overlay on a Chart Plotter

The latest trend in full-sized chartplotters is to combine them with the radar display. It is possible to split the screen so that the chartplotter display uses one-half the screen and the radar the other. It's also possible on many to overlay the radar display on the chartplotter display, so that the two are superimposed. To do this requires a high-speed electronic fluxgate compass.

I find that for collision avoidance purposes the overlaid screen is too cluttered and prefer a separate radar display. However, for the purposes of navigation and pilotage, the overlaid radar has considerable merit.

For the overlay, the radar echoes are often coloured magenta, which is mostly not present on the cartography so the radar echoes stand out well. The radar echoes should correspond with the cartography and this makes identifying the shoreline and navigation marks much easier. Any radar echo that doesn't register with a charted feature is likely to be a ship.

Chartplotter with radar overlay

Radar echo of shoreline registers with charted shoreline

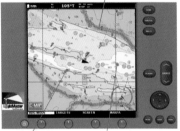

Radar echo of buoy registers with buoy   Echo with no charted feature is probably a ship

Do the radar echoes correspond with the chart?

Very large chart error

With radar overlay, the chart error is very obvious.

Any error in the cartography or GPS will become apparent, because the radar will not agree with the chart. The radar is correct!

Setting up Your Radar

Setting up your radar properly is very important. Most sets have some form of automatic adjustment of some important functions, they're getting better, but you can always do better yourself if you know what to do.

A good illustration of this occurred when I was on a long passage in flat calm seas, and with little else to do, I was playing with the radar. Having adjusted everything very carefully, I noticed some fast moving echoes ahead, but saw nothing on the water. I looked up a little and there were some seabirds (Gannets) flying round ahead and it was their echoes that I could see. I then set all the controls to automatic and their echoes disappeared!

B.R.G.T.

This simple mnemonic should help.

- B – adjust the *brightness* to suit the lighting conditions around you. On an LCD display, you'll need to adjust the *Contrast* instead. This is not adjusting the signal, just making the screen readable.
- R – now select an intermediate *range*, about 4 to 6 miles is good, as long as there are targets within range. Some authors suggest setting gain before setting range, but ideally you need to set the gain at an intermediate range, so why not set the range, first?
- G – adjust the *gain* to give good strong returns, but don't overdo it. As a rule of thumb, on a CRT set, adjust until there are speckles (noise) on the screen and then reduce the gain until they are only just visible. On a LCD screen, adjust the gain until you have speckles and then reduce the gain until there are just no speckles visible. If you are not confident about this set the gain to automatic, but you will loose a bit of performance.
- T – now adjust the *tuning*. Ideally the set will have a tuning meter – you adjust the tuning up and down until you have the maximum number of bars visible. Some modern sets don't have this facility, and adjusting tuning manually may be difficult for the inexperienced, in which case you'd better leave it set to automatic. The tuning control adjusts the receiver frequency so that it's the same as the transmitter frequency. The transmitter magnetron changes frequency as it heats up, so it should be adjusted again after about 10 minutes. The magnetron also changes temperature as the range is changed and needs to be checked again. If you find that automatic tuning gives a good display, you may as well use automatic, although again, you may loose a little performance.

Radar Used for Collision Avoidance

This is a book all about practical navigation. You'll find other books telling how to use radar for collision avoidance (Wiley Nautical's Radar Companion' is one).

However, I think it appropriate to remind readers that special rules come into force when vessels are not in sight of one another and conflicting traffic can be seen only on radar.

'Colregs'

The normal 'rules of the road' governing 'stand on' and 'give-way' vessels apply only to 'vessels in sight of one another' – rule 11.

Conduct of Vessels in Restricted Visibility

Rule 7 b

Proper use shall be made of radar equipment if fitted and operational, including long range scanning to obtain early warning of risk of collision and radar plotting or equivalent systematic observation of detected objects.

Rule 7 c

Assumptions shall not be made on the basis of scanty information, especially scanty radar information.

Rule 19 d

A vessel which detects by radar alone, the presence of another vessel shall determine if a close-quarters situation is developing and/or risk of collision exists. If so, she shall take avoiding action in ample time, provided that when such action consists of an alteration of course, so far as possible the following shall be avoided:

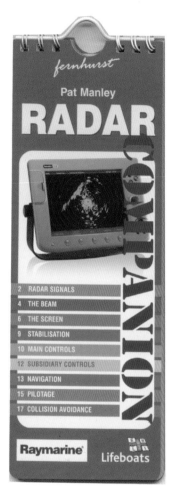

- an alteration of course to port for a vessel forward of the beam, other than for a vessel being overtaken;

- an alteration of course towards a vessel abeam or abaft the beam.

Rule 19 e

...or which cannot avoid a close–quarters situation with another vessel forward of her beam, shall reduce her speed to the minimum at which she can be kept on her course. She shall, if necessary, take all her way off...

'Rule 19'

Rule 19 of the 'Colregs' can be summarised in the following diagram – there is no stand on vessel and *all* vessels are give-way vessels – and if you are going to use your radar in restricted visibility, you *must* be aware of it. Remember that you can slow down or stop as well as turn.

If you need to make a turn to avoid a close
quarters situation, this diagram tells you
which way to turn. Take extra care in the
ambiguous zone the area between 'forward
of abeam' and 'abeam'.

The 'essence' of rule 19

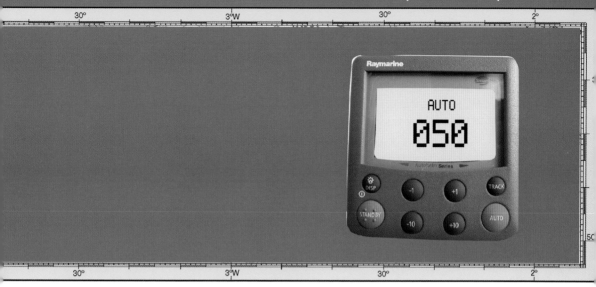

Autopilots

Types of Autopilot

Using the Autopilot

An autopilot can reduce the workload on the helmsman and navigator. For longer short-handed passages, it can allow proper time for navigation and pilotage.

13.1. Types of Autopilot

There are two basic types of autopilots:

- A simple autopilot, which maintains a set compass heading.
  - This may have no heading display and will 'take up' the heading the boat is on when the autopilot is switched *on*. Heading is altered with 'left and right' keys and the heading will be monitored using the steering compass.

- Some will have a heading display, will again take up the heading at 'switch on', have left and right keys, but the heading can now be monitored on the autopilot display and checked against the steering compass.
- An autopilot linked to the navigation instruments, which can automatically take you to a waypoint or even follow a complete route.
  - This type will have a remote 'flux gate' compass, a heading display and keys and displays allowing a route to be followed.

Personally, I do not advocate coupling the autopilot to the navigation system to automatically follow a route for the following reasons:

- With the autopilot making constant alterations of heading to maintain the cross track error to a minimum, the navigator has absolutely no idea of the compass course being followed, and cannot revert to 'DR' navigation if needed.
- Steering a compass-linked course allows any compass errors to become obvious. 'Coupling up' to the route or waypoint means that a constant compass course is not being steered and any compass error is difficult to assess.
- A short-lived GPS error can cause the boat to suddenly veer off course – I have witnessed such incidents.
- The helmsman/navigator loses positional awareness of the operation of the boat.
- Steering a compass-linked course allows the navigator to assess the effect of leeway and the accuracy of the tidal current predictions – essential if he needs to revert to DR navigation.

13.2. Using the Autopilot

- The autopilot when not being used will be in the 'standby' mode.
- When set to 'auto' mode, the heading can be adjusted to that required by the navigator/pilot.
- By monitoring the bearing and distance to waypoint and the cross track error, the heading can be adjusted to either regain track or go directly to the waypoint if that is a safe course of action.

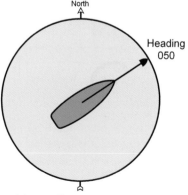

Manually steering 050

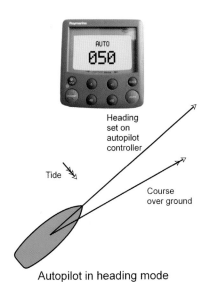

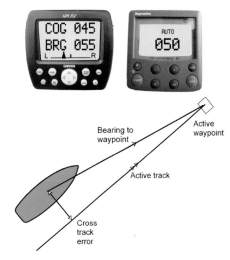

Autopilot in heading mode

Cross track error to an active waypoint

- If you want to couple up to an active waypoint, then 'Track' or 'Nav' is selected. If you are already on the correct track to the waypoint, the autopilot will steer such headings as will maintain the cross track error at zero.

- If you are not on the correct track when you select 'Track' or 'Nav', the autopilot will immediately turn the boat to regain the correct track. You need to be aware which way the boat will turn and by how many degrees, in case there's another boat or obstruction in the way. When the cross track error has been reduced to zero, the boat will again be turned (so keep monitoring what is happening) and then steered to maintain zero cross track error.

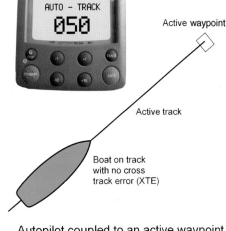

Autopilot coupled to an active waypoint

- If you have 'coupled up' to a route, you need to be aware of what will happen when you get to the next waypoint. The majority of autopilots will give an audio warning that the waypoint has been reached, and if no action is taken, will revert to heading mode and continue on the last heading. They will not make an unsupervised turn to the next waypoint as this could cause a collision with any nearby boats.

If you do decide to use navigation mode, you must continue to 'navigate the boat' mentally and not be distracted.

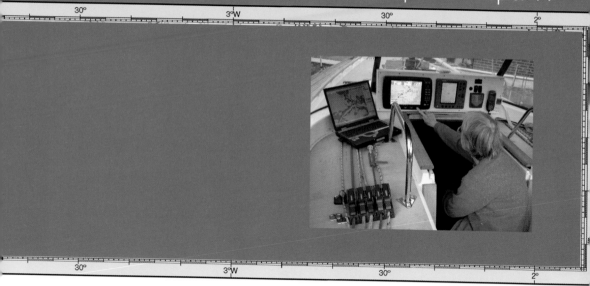

Personal Computers

I've been using a personal computer (PC) for some navigation activities on my boat since about 1999. It isn't essential by any means, but it's very useful and I enjoy using it.

Only users who have never experienced a computer crash would ever dream of using a PC as their sole means of navigation.

What Type of PC?

With the advent of 'on board entertainment PCs' there's a temptation to use a desktop or miniaturised desktop computer for the job. That's fine when you are running on mains or generator power, but running off an inverter can cause unwanted shutdowns and I wouldn't recommend it when you are using it for navigation. I believe that a laptop PC is a better bet. It can be run from a smaller inverter or a 12 volts adaptor, but should always be able to fall back on its internal battery if the external power fails. The hard drive in a laptop will be more robust that a desktop version and the cost of a 'ruggedised' laptop is prohibitive.

Unless you want to make use of the three-dimensional (3D) capabilities of some chart-plotting software, a powerful PC is not required. My boat PC runs Windows 98 and has a 475 megahertz CPU and only 64 megabytes of random access memory (RAM). It does an excellent job, but wouldn't run the latest version of my software, which does need more computing power, but a P4 processor and 256 megabytes of RAM should be fine. Check with the software vendor. If you really need to use the fantastic 3D capabilities, then a high-spec machine with a separate graphics card is essential.

There's much to be said for a computer that is never connected to the Internet, as it then wouldn't suffer from a virus.

What Make of Chart-Plotting Software?

This depends very much on personal choice, the depth of your pocket and what you intend to use it for. You need to consider what features you require:

- Some software is pretty basic, allowing a route to be constructed but not planned using tidal stream data. Others allow full tidal planning and weather routing, constructing sailing polar diagrams, using lay lines when tacking and more. Most software is somewhere in between.
- There are two types of electronic charts; raster and vector. Their capabilities are very different and some software will not be compatible with vector charts.
- Automatic Identification System (AIS) can be shown on some systems.

- A radar overlay is possible with some systems, though this will normally be restricted to a specific radar.
- Some systems allow waypoint and route data to be uploaded to a global positioning system (GPS) or chartplotter.
- Some systems allow the software to control the boat's autopilot.
- Some systems allow the use of chartplotter memory cards, which can be used in the PC and then transferred to your chartplotter.

What Type of Electronic Charts?

Of considerable importance is what type of electronic charts can be used.

Raster Charts

- Raster charts are electronic clones of a paper chart.
- They look just like its equivalent paper chart.
- They should be viewed at a specific scale.

UKHO raster chart

– scanned from the UKHO paper chart

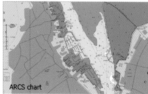

Viewed at the correct 'zoom' for the scale of the chart – 1:3,500 – obtained by using the 1:1 control icon – the detail on a chart of a given scale is always the same because there is only one layer

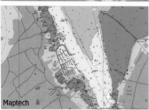

Maptech raster chart

– scanned from the UKHO paper chart

Over-zoomed – no extra detail but the chart becomes 'pixelated'

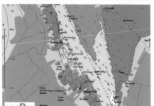

SeaPro 'livechart' vector chart

– redrawn using data from UKHO paper chart

Over-zoomed, even more giving, even greater pixelation

Raster and vector charts

Raster zooming

Vector Charts

- Vector charts are redrawn completely by the electronic chart cartographers.
- There are many layers, each with different types of data, and these layers may be switched on or off either by the user or automatically as you zoom in or out.
- Photographs, pilots, information, etc. can all be embedded.
- Errors may be introduced in the cartography during the copying process.
- Vector charts may not look exactly like their paper counterparts.
- Vector charts bring huge flexibility to the system.

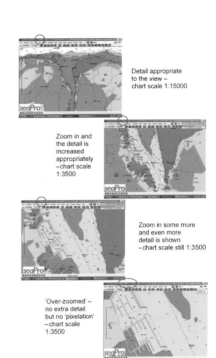

Detail appropriate to the view – chart scale 1:15000

Zoom in and the detail is increased appropriately –chart scale 1:3500

Zoom in some more and even more detail is shown – chart scale still 1:3500

'Over-zoomed' – no extra detail but no 'pixelation' –chart scale 1:3500

Zooming in on a vector chart

Electronic Charts for PC Based Chartplotters

In the past, each software provider has produced their own electronic charts, but this is getting prohibitively expensive. There is now a tendency to use third party electronic charting, especially as there is now an international standard for electronic cartography.

Professional Cartography

Most new commercial vessels use electronic chart displays on the bridge, and where legislation controls the type of equipment used, all electronic charts will be according to the S57 (vector) International Standard.

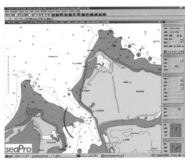

S 57 chart

Leisure Cartography

Electronic charts used in the leisure sector are much more variable and will depend on the software provider, some using only one sort of chart and others able to use several, including S57. Probably, the ideal is the ability to use multiple types of charts, including those used by dedicated chartplotters, such as C-Map and Navionics. The user then gets

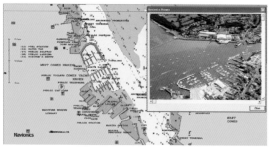

This Navionics vector chart used on many chartplotters, can also be used with seaPro's PC based chart plotting software. It has many enhancements for the leisure boater including photographs of marinas, etc. Full seaPro passage planning can be made using the Navionics charts.

Navionics charts on a PC

the value added facilities including photographs and marina information, valuable to some boat owners.

Selecting the Software

A visit to the chart-plotting software vendor's web site should show you what facilities are available. There are often several versions to choose from, extra facilities costing more money. Upgrades from one version to another are usually possible.

You need to ask yourself; will the computer be

- The only chartplotter on the boat?
- Used only for constructing a route?
- Used for planning a route – including tidal planning with best time of departure and track made good over the ground?
- Used to construct/plan a route and send the route to a GPS or a chartplotter?
- Used to combine with wind forecasts over the period of the route to plan the best route to take account of the varying wind direction and strength.
- Used to display 'lay lines', tacking angles, sailing 'polars', etc. to optimise best navigate the route of a sailing yacht.
- Is it compatible with the chart type of my choice – raster or vector?
- Can it be used with my chartplotter's memory card?

Constructing a Route

Constructing a route on a PC based chartplotter is usually simplicity itself. The cursor is placed over the position that you wish to have a waypoint, you click the mouse, move onto the next position and click again, continuing to the end of the route. The only problem is that the screen size will limit the amount of detail that you can see, though this is much better than the average dedicated chartplotter. For safety, you'll need to zoom in and out and pan along the route to examine it along its length to ensure that it runs into no dangers.

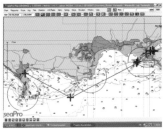

Click the mouse where you wish to insert waypoints to make up a route.

PC route 1

Zoom in and check each portion of the route for safety.

PC route 2

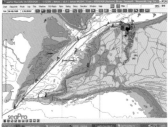

Zoom in and out as necessary and pan along the route.

PC route 3

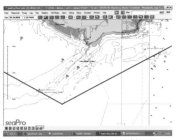

Continue along the route at an appropriate zoom.

PC route 4

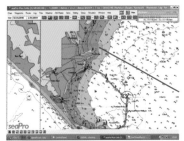

Until you reach the end of the route.

PC route 5

Some chart-plotting software, such as seaPro, allows various departure times to be investigated to give the shortest time on route, using the

Planning departure time

The plan overview shows course to steer for end elapsed time for each leg and ETA destination for the selected departure time.

Route plan

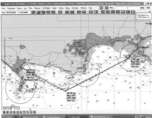

Once the route has been calculated, the track over the ground is displayed as a dashed line and the leg details may also be displayed on the chart if desired.

Route plan details

With a long 'cross-tide' passage, the cross track displacement of the ground track will be significant. Chartplotting software that displays the ground track is at a distinct advantage over those that don't.

Display of ground track

The more comprehensive software is then able to calculate the time en route according to the time and date of departure, allowing for the tidal flow. The course to steer and the elapsed time on each leg are also calculated.

Even better, some software allows the track over the ground to be displayed. This is invaluable, especially where the course is predominantly across the tidal flow, as the cross track displacement may be considerable and could run the boat into danger.

Sailing Yacht Route Planning

A sailing boat's speed depends on the wind strength and direction. You can assume a single average speed and calculate the route using this. If the wind is from ahead, then you'll have to tack down this route and the plan will be very inaccurate.

Sailing Polars

Sailing polars are the performance data for various sail plans, in different wind strengths at different angle to the wind. Initially, they are the designer's predictions, but these are then modified in the light of sea trials.

The polar shown in the diagram is a default polar diagram from Euronav's seaPro chart-plotting software. This can be edited manually and on some versions of the software may be automatically updated as you sail. It is the performance data from these polars that is used with the forecast winds to produce the weather routing sail plans.

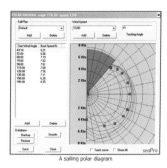

A sailing polar diagram

Allowing for the Forecast Wind

Some chart-plotting software allows you to insert the forecast wind into the plan, which will then calculate the probable boat speeds in the various wind strengths and directions, telling you when you should tack, using the boat's actual performance data (sailing polars). Good software will allow for the changing tidal flows as well.

An alternative to manually inserting the various wind conditions is to download a weather file from the Internet. Most weather routing software uses the standard GRIB

Wind data can be inserted manually, changing at intervals of your choice for the duration of the voyage, allowing the most advantageous route to be chosen according to both wind and tide.

Weather routing 1

The weather route's tacking points and courses to steer can be calculated.

Weather routing 2

The grib file (weather) can be displayed. If the grib file is for a forecast period of 60 hours, the wind direction and other data if available can be shown for various time intervals.

Midnight GRIB

(GRIdded Binary) format and the files cover a specific forecast time period, giving, say, the conditions every 4 hours for the following 72 hours.

GRIB files are available from various sources. Some are free and have minimal, but sufficient data and some are by subscription. Subscription data will be on a much smaller grid basis and contain added data such as wave heights, temperature, cloud cover and more.

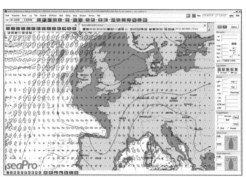

The wind pattern for 24 hours later
24 hour GRIB

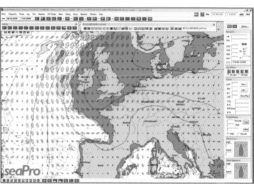

The wind pattern for 42 hours later
42 hour GRIB

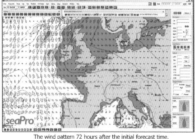

The wind pattern 72 hours after the initial forecast time.
72 hour GRIB

Weather files (grib files) can be down loaded from the internet and the software then allows the winds from these files to be used to calculate the best route to be calculated

The fastest route

If your software supports weather routing, the vendor's web site will have links to various sources of GRIB files.

Sending the Route to the GPS

Although the PC will almost certainly have the boat's position input from a GPS set, which allows the navigation to be carried out using the PC, it's a very good idea to transmit the route data from the PC to the GPS. In this case, should the PC fail, the route will still be available in the GPS to allow continued electronic navigation. If you are using a dedicated electronic chartplotter, then the route, once constructed on the PC, can be transferred to the chartplotter.

Compatibility of Route Transfer

Unfortunately, some GPS and chartplotter manufacturers use their own protocol, rather than the industry standard NMEA. The PC chart-plotting software uses NMEA sentences to receive GPS and other data, and also uses NMEA to transmit information back to the GPS/chartplotter. At the time of writing, Garmin GPS and chartplotters wouldn't accept route transfers in NMEA. It's possible to send individual waypoints, but you will have to string these together yourself in the Garmin GPS/chartplotter. There seems to be no problem in chartplotters which use third party cartography, such as C-Map and Navionics.

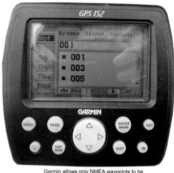

Garmin allows only NMEA waypoints to be transferred, not the whole route.

Garmin transfer

AIS on a PC

Some PC chart-plotting software is able to display AIS information. All received AIS targets are displayed in real time on the chart, with their tracks, course over ground, and with some software a vector based on its rate of turn.

With AIS switched on, all received vessels are displayed. Data boxes show vital information.

AIS display 1

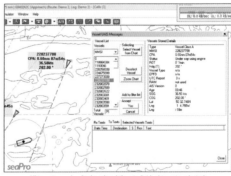

All targets can be displayed and then individual targets selected to display all its transmitted data.

AIS display 2

If the closest point of approach (CPA) becomes less than the user defined value, the target blinks, an audio warning sounds and the display includes the value of the CPA and the elapsed time until the CPA.

A list of all the targets can be displayed on the screen, all the data for each target can be viewed or alternatively if a target is clicked, then its data can be displayed.

Individual targets can be 'clicked' to display all its data.

AI display 3

Radar on a PC

Several versions of the PC chart-plotting software are able to act as a radar display. These require a special radar scanner, rather than taking signals from the usual scanner provided with a conventional system. The scanner output is sent directly to the PC and all control of the radar is carried out from the PC software.

The radar display can be 'whole screen' radar only, 'split screen' alongside the chartplotter display, or 'superimposed' on the chart.

Stand-Alone Radar

The radar display fills the PC monitor screen and all the radar controls are operated using the computer mouse. Because all the controls are visible and not immersed in various menu levels, operating the radar is very straightforward – much easier than a modern leisure radar.

The radar may be operated in north-up or head-up modes at a click of the mouse button.

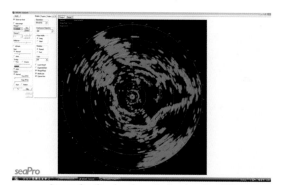

Range 2 miles, head-up display, heading 228

Split Screen Radar

When the PC chart-plotting software is in use, the radar may be displayed in its own window on the PC screen alongside the chart-plotting software. Alternatively, it may be displayed in its own window on the top of the chart-plotting software.

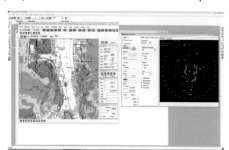
Radar and chart-plotting software side-by-side

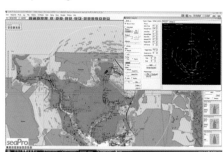
Radar window on chart window

Superimposed Radar

The radar display may be superimposed onto the chart display. This has two major advantages:

- Certainty of identifying large cartographic or GPS errors. You need to know where you are relative to the land (and its dangers). Only the radar will tell you this. The accompanying diagram shows a deliberately induced GPS error, which would have been invisible had we not used superimposed radar. Another interesting error which showed up when preparing this section of the book was an apparent angular error in the superimposed image. This was probably due to some form of compass or radar alignment error.

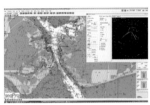

A deliberate GPS error of 1000 metres North and 1000 metres West has been introduced. On the chart plotter alone this would not have been seen. With the radar overlaid on the chart, the error is immediately obvious - the radar must be correct and the GPS or cartography must be wrong.

GPS/cartographic error

- Ease of identifying topographical features on the radar. Because the radar can't see around corners, it's often difficult to match the radar image to the chart. Superimposed radar overcomes this difficulty, especially if there are extensive mud flats which show up

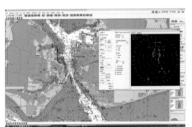

With the error removed our position is correct. The saw-tooth red track line shows where deliberate errors of 300, 600 and 1000 metres were introduced.

The correct picture

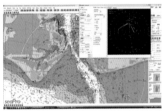

Superimposed radar with split screen. Heading 170, radar range 2 miles. There is some evidence of a compass error as the return for the NW and NE shores appear to be misaligned by about 6 degrees.

Superimposed radar and split screen

Heading 040, radar range 0.75 mile. The magenta lines show where I have rotated the radar image through 9 degrees to align it with the directions of the shorelines. This error could be due to compass deviation, the radar not being aligned with the boat's centreline or one set of data being based on magnetic and the other true.

Compass error

Radar superimposed on chart, North-up, heading 230, radar range set at 2 miles. Software has matched the radar range to the scale of the chart and converted the radar image to North-up.

Superimposed radar

on the radar at low water. Also, superimposition sometimes makes it clearer which are boats rather than navigation marks.

PC Radar for Pilotage

The usefulness of superimposed radar for pilotage can't be understated, except for one problem; the screen must be in the view of the pilot, who should be in full view of his surroundings, that is able to look outside.

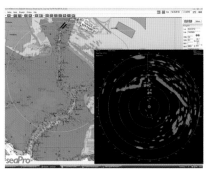

Superimposed radar and split screen radar being used for pilotage. This utilises two completely different tools with different sources of data, one of which is the land itself, giving much greater confidence.

Split screen pilotage

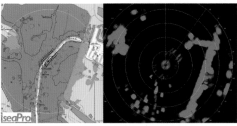

With the radar set to 0.25 mile range, very accurate pilotage is possible.

Accurate pilotage

GPS error of about 30 metres (the lower of the two traces) would have made pilotage in fog dangerous without radar, which would have shown up the error. If you look carefully at the previous diagram, this difference between the GPS position and the superimposed radar position can be seen.

GPS error

Used at a suitable chart scale on the plotter and a very low range on the radar, then any discrepancy between GPS, cartography and radar can be seen. Provided the radar is set up properly, its view of the world is correct.

We can see in the accompanying diagrams that the ideal is to have a superimposed chart/radar in one half of the screen and the stand alone radar in the other. Obviously, the bigger the screen the better.

This technique can also be used with a radar superimposed chartplotter, but often the screen is too small for accurate use.

PC Radar for Collision Avoidance

Personally, I do not like superimposed radar for collision avoidance as I find it too confusing. I would use split screen radar or standalone radar for this purpose.

Navtex on a PC

Dedicated Navtex receivers are left in standby mode for the whole time so that they will receive all the messages, which are displayed on demand by the user. The PC can be linked to a Navtex receiver, but for the best use the PC will need to be left running all the time, which is probably not the way you will use an onboard PC.

Navtex window in view – you can scroll through the messages.

Navtex

Tides on a PC

Various forms of tidal software are available for use on a PC, some of them 'stand alone' and some integrated with the chart-plotting software.

Tidal Flow

Tidal flow data may be integrated with the chart-plotting software and allows both strategic and tactical planning if the software supports planning.

• It is used in the initial route planning to obtain the time of departure that gives the fastest passage.

Tidal flow can be displayed on some chart plotting software
The flow is given in real time and as the passage progresses,
the tide vectors change accordingly. The time can be scrolled
forward or backwards over any time span to investigate
various tactical options

Tidal flow

- It is used for passage planning when wind against tide is of consideration.
- It is used for passage and re-routing planning where an ebb tide would preclude entry or a flood tide would preclude departure.
- It is used en route for tactical considerations, such as avoiding tide races, etc.

Tidal Heights

Tidal height software is available as standalone software or may be integrated with the chart-plotting software.

Standalone Software

Completely independent of any chart-plotting software, tidal height information is available in both numerical and graphical format. The number of tidal stations and geographical area covered will depend on the software used. Some software will also run on hand-held computers (PDAs).

Built-In Software

Some chart-plotting software has built-in tidal height data. As well as having a list of tidal stations, you may also be able to click on tidal station logos which will then display the real time data for that station. Other dates and times can also be chosen for planning purposes.

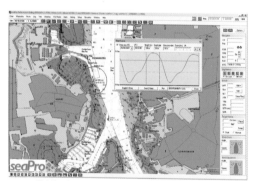

Tidal height curves are often available within chart-plotting software, sometimes for many secondary ports as well as standard ports.

Tidal height curves

Connecting to the Boat's Systems

The Industry standard communication language is NMEA 0183, with NMEA 2000 becoming common. Different manufacturers use their own languages as well, but any communication with a PC will be in one of the NMEA standards.

Instrument Wiring

Where a number of different instrument systems are mixed, it is notoriously difficult to get them to interface satisfactorily. Using a 'multiplexer' to combine the instrument outputs into one combined NMEA data stream should solve any problems.

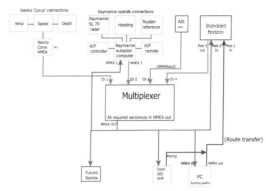

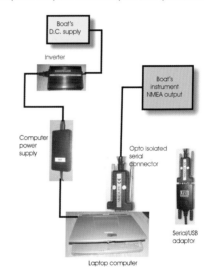

Added complexity requires a multiplexer to ensure only one 'talker' per channel.

Wired Connection

The boat's NMEA output is in the form of an RS232 connection, which connects directly to the PCs serial port. Most modern PCs have no serial port connection, so you will need a serial/USB adaptor, some of which seem unreliable. One proven to work with your software may be a better, though more expensive, option. A particular snag with using a serial/USB interface with Windows 2000, Windows XP and Windows Vista is that your computer is likely to think that the NMEA data are mouse inputs, so you will lose control of your cursor and be unable to use your computer! You can modify your registry (Microsoft Knowledge Base Article - Q131976 http://support.microsoft.com/default.aspx?scid=kb; [LN];Q131976), but the safest way is to ensure that you connect your computer to the live NMEA output before you switch your computer on.

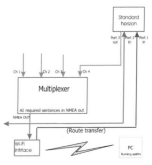

Wireless Connection

A convenient way to supply your PC with NMEA data is via a Wi-Fi connection. The NMEA data is fed to a Wi-Fi transmitter, which then transmits all the NMEA data to a Wi-Fi enabled PC. The PC can now be used anywhere on the boat, including the cockpit, and there are no problems with losing control of the mouse cursor.

Wi-Fi link between NMEA and computer

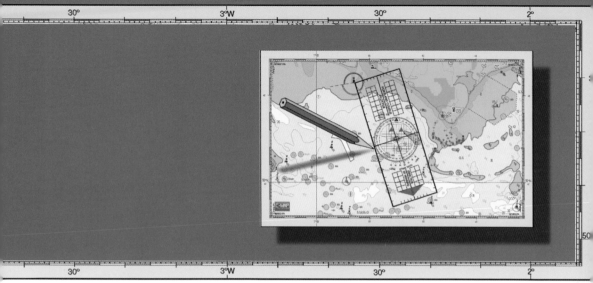

Deduced Reckoning and Estimated Position

DR Navigation

Estimated Position

Leeway

Error in EP

EP with Multiple Headings

When aids to navigation are in short supply, due to equipment failure or lack of any aids, the navigator must resort to traditional methods of navigation.

DR Navigation

DR navigation is the method of deducing your position using only heading steered and distance run. This is 'deduced navigation' and is often known, erroneously in my opinion, as 'dead reckoning' rather than 'ded. reckoning', but anyway it's commonly called 'DR'.

If you know where you started from, the direction in which the boat has been travelling and the distance travelled, it's very easy to plot where you are on a chart. This makes no allowance for tide or wind, so is only of use in relatively calm conditions where there is little or no tide.

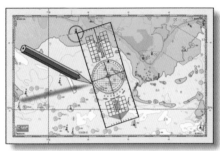

DR course steered – 165 (T)

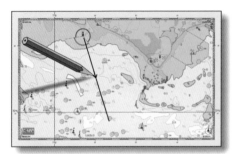

DR – One arrow for water track

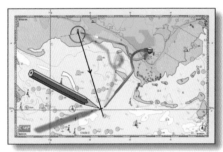

DR distance run – 6 miles

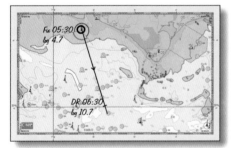

DR position – Positions labled

The course steered must be converted from a Compass course to a True course by applying deviation and variation. The distance run is taken from the speed log, which should have been calibrated. If it under reads, you would have travelled further than you thought and may be standing into danger.

Estimated Position

The *estimated position* (EP) is determined by applying any tidal and wind effects to the DR position. We'll look first at applying only tide.

We will need to establish in what direction and at what speed the tide has been pushing the boat for the time since we last knew our position. This is obtained from the tidal atlas. If, for instance, the last 'fix' was 1 hour ago, we will need to examine the tidal

atlas page for that particular hour. As we will
be transferring the direction using our plotter,
we need only 'line it up', without actually
reading the direction. We will, however, need
to determine its speed by noting if the day's
tidal range is neaps, springs or in between.

Now we will mark the direction of the tidal
flow on the chart, using the plotter. Then we
can mark the distance the tide will have carried
us since the last fix. The symbol for an EP is a
triangle, to distinguish it from a fix.

The resulting position is our estimated
position. We must mark on the chart the total

The tidal atlas diagram from 05:30 until 06:30

mean tidal stream direction

distance run and the time of the EP, so that anyone looking at the chart will have all the
information they need at a glance.

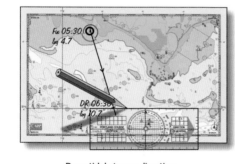

Draw tidal stream direction

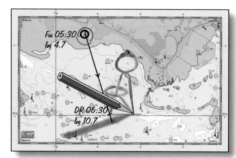

Mark the length of the tidal vector

EP at 06:30

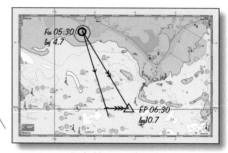

Probable ground track

If we are interested in where the boat had actually travelled over the ground since the
last fix, then all we have to do is join the fix position to the EP. This is the average track
that we have made good, though because it has used the average tide for the period, it
won't represent the true picture exactly.

Leeway

Wind can blow the boat sideways through the water. Boats will be affected in different ways according to their shape, both above and below the water, the direction and strength of the wind, the boat's speed and the direction of the wind relative to the boat. It's normal to allow for 0 degrees, 5 degrees or 10 degrees according to conditions. Leeway can be estimated by measuring the direction of the wake of the boat

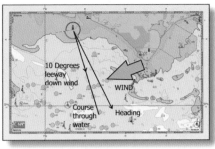

Leeway

with a hand-bearing compass and comparing it with the boat's heading. The boat will be blown 'down wind' from the boats heading. It's a good idea to always sketch a wind arrow on your chart so that you apply leeway in the correct direction.

Error in EP

Because an EP relies on information that may not be as accurate as we would like, it's normal to allow for an error of up to 10% of the distance run when working out our next course. Draw a circle of radius 10% of distance run since the last reliable fix centred on the EP. Assume that your position is in a position, within the circle, nearest to danger. In other words 'navigate the circle' rather than the boat.

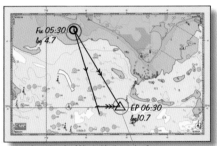

Actual position should be inside the circle of error, which has a radius of 10% of the distance run.

Ten percent circle of error

EP with Multiple Headings

You don't need to work out an EP at each change of heading. Provided that you note the log distance at each change of heading, you can run a series of DR positions and insert the tide or tides at the end when you are ready.

This will not give you an indication of the ensuing ground track but give a good EP.

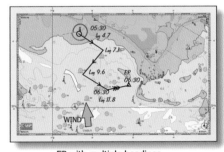

EP with multiple headings

Standard Symbols

We must use the standard symbols for our chart work so that any other person will understand what we have plotted.

- The course through the water has *one* arrow.
- The course over the ground has *two* arrows.
- The tide has *three* arrows.

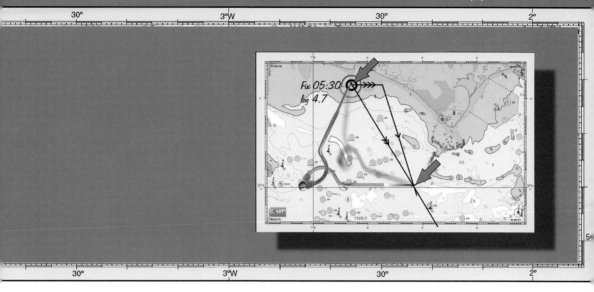

Course to Steer

Where Do You Want to Go?

What Time Interval Do You Choose?

Draw in the Tide

Draw in the Boat Speed

Ground Speed

Comparison with EP

Unless you are operating in tideless and windless waters, you will need to calculate a course to steer to get from A to B. If you just steer the direct track between the two points, the wind and tide will take you in a different direction.

149

At the first sight, it may seem a little complicated, but practice a few times and it should become second nature. One essential reminder is that unlike estimated positions (EPs), the tide comes first, not last!

In order to strive for clarity, the first diagram shows the completed vector triangle, while the subsequent diagrams show the step-by-step method.

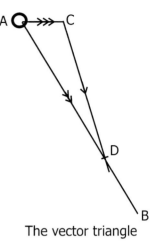

The vector triangle

Where Do You Want to Go?

- Draw a line from your starting point (A) to and *beyond* your destination (B). This is so that if the trip takes more than the nominal time you have *guessed*, the line will be long enough. Because this is the ground track, it must have two arrows.

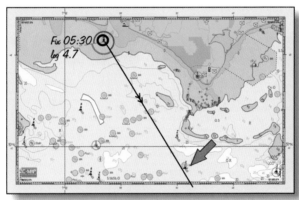

Distance from 05:30 fix to destination is 8.3 miles
At 6 knots it will take about 1 hour 24 minutes

The required ground track

- Measure the distance from A to B.
- Using the probable speed through the water, calculate the estimated time taken to cover the distance A – B. Distance divided by speed gives time in hours. Multiply by 60 to get the time in minutes.
- This time is used to form the basis of the calculation of tidal effect.

What Time Interval Do You Choose?

The 'velocity' triangle you are going to construct must have all three sides representing the *same* period of time. Since we are going to start off with a guessed time, it makes sense to use an easily handled time interval, which will normally be 1 hour. However, sometimes we can use half an hour or even one and a half hours, depending on whether the triangle will fit the paper chart or not.

Draw in the Tide

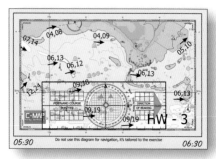

- Transfer the tidal direction from the tidal atlas to the chart, with the tidal flow (three arrows) pointing away from your starting point A.

- Estimate the tidal speed with reference to 'neaps or springs'.

- Mark the tidal vector with how far the tide will take the boat in the time interval of the triangle (C). That is for a 1-hour triangle, use 1 hour of tide; for a half-an-hour triangle, use half an hour of tide.

The tidal atlas diagram from 05:30 until 06:30
Estimate the tidal stream

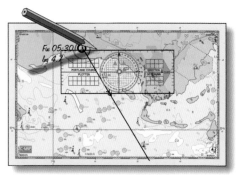

Draw direction of tidal stream

Mark length of tidal vector

Draw in the Boat Speed

- Open up your dividers (or compasses) to the distance that the boat will travel through the water in the time of the triangle. That is 1 hour of boat speed for a 1-hour triangle or half an hour of boat speed for a half-an-hour triangle.

- Mark this distance from the end of the tidal vector (C) to a position where it cuts the line joining A to B and beyond (D). Give it one arrow.

Mark off the distance travelled through the water in 1 hour from the end of the tidal vector to the ground track line.
The distance travelled in 1 hour

- You now have a vector triangle, one side of which has the tidal effect for a given period (1 hour or half an hour), the boat speed effect for the same time interval and therefore the third side must represent the distance travelled over the ground for that same time interval.

Course to steer vector

- The direction of the boat speed vector from the end of the tide (C) to where it cuts the ground track at (D) is the course to steer if there is no leeway.

Course to steer = 165 (T) 168 (M)

Measure course to Steer

When calculating course to steer, we will have to 'steer into wind' to make good the course we wish to steer through the water.

Leeway (CTS)

- If there is any leeway, you must steer *into* wind by the estimated leeway to ensure that the path through the water is in the direction C to D.

Ground Speed

- Measure the length of the ground speed side of the triangle (A – D). This is the distance travelled over the ground in the time interval of the triangle. If it's a 1-hour triangle, then this *is* the ground speed. If it's a half-an-hour triangle, then this is the distance travelled in half an hour, so double it to get the ground speed.

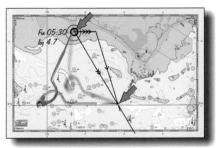

Measure ground speed = 6.7 knots
Distance to destination = 8.3 miles
Time to destination   = 1 hour 14 minutes
ETA destination   = 06:44

Calculate ETA

- Using this ground speed and the distance from your starting point to your destination (A – B) you can work out your estimated time of arrival (ETA). Distance divided by speed gives the elapsed time in hours. Multiply by 60 to get the time in minutes. Add this to the time you started to get your ETA.

Comparison with EP

- Have a look at the accompanying diagram 'DR and CTS' and you will see that the two triangles will bring you to the same point on the chart for the same time interval. A reassurance that the initial 'guessing' was just a tool to get the correct answer.

Our EP after 1 hour will be the same position as that found when calculating course to steer for 1 hour. This is logical as all the data are the same.

DR and CTS

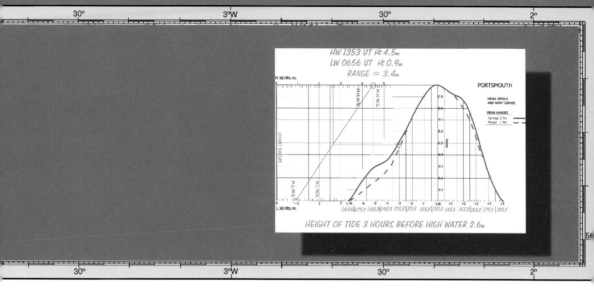

Tidal Heights and Tidal Streams

Atmospheric Pressure Corrections

Tide Tables

UKHO Tidal Predictions

SHOM Tidal Predictions

Tidal Streams

It is possible to obtain heights of tide for any day using 'online' sources. However, the navigator is often forced into a position where there's a need to calculate the height of tide at a particular time manually. There are a number of different methods of doing this, some more accurate than others.

Where the tidal curve is of sine waveform, the rule of twelfths, as discussed in Chapter 5, will serve well. If, however, the curve is 'skewed', that is not symmetrical, or even worse and has deformities, then better methods are required, if an accurate prediction is required. It's essential to reiterate, though, that these are only predictions. The atmospheric pressure and wind can make significant differences, and the navigator needs to exercise caution when using calculated height of tide.

Atmospheric Pressure Corrections

- A pressure of 10 millibars (hPa) above 1013 millibars will depress the tide level by 10 centimetres (4 inches).
- A pressure of 10 millibars below 1013 millibars will raise the tide level by 10 centimetres (4 inches).

Tide Tables

Tide tables are published for most major ports. These give the times and heights of high and low water for every day of the year. Where there's no commercial pressure to publish tables, tables of differences may be available so that the results obtained from the major port (standard ports) can be modified to allow calculations to be made for these 'secondary ports'.

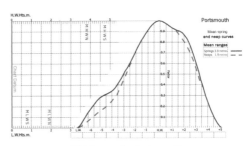

Tidal differences at Bembridge

Tidal curve for Portsmouth

UKHO Tidal Predictions

In many parts of the United Kingdom, the tidal curve is skewed, and along parts of England's south coast, the curve is far from smooth, especially due to the flow up and down the channel and the influence of the Isle of Wight.

The UKHO has developed a graphical method of finding the height of tide at any time on any day of the year. This allows for the different shapes of the tidal curve which may apply to spring and neap tides.

The easiest way to describe the use of the UKHO method is by following an example, which will entail the use of the curve for a standard port, applying the differences for a secondary port and then using the curve to find the height of tide at a particular time.

Get Today's Information

We will find the height of tide at Portsmouth at 10:53 BST on 4th July.

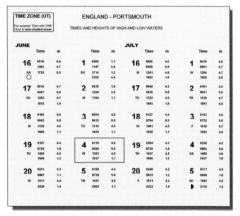

HW 1353 UT Ht 4.5 metres
LW 1917 UT Ht 1.1 metres
Tidal data for 4th July – Portsmouth

- Look up the times and heights of HW and LW for Portsmouth on 4th July.

- Apply any correction for local time (in this case add 1 hour for BST) and write the time of HW in the HW box at the bottom of the curve.

- Fill in the other time boxes along the bottom of the curve.

- Mark the height of HW on the top tidal height scale.

- Mark the height of LW on the bottom tidal height scale.

- Join these two points with a straight line.

- The heights of HW and LW can be compared with the heights of MHWS and MHWN and of MLWS and MLWN to see what part of the curve needs to be used where there are differences between spring and neap tides.

- Draw a vertical line from the time required on the bottom of the curve (10:53, which equals 3 hours before high water) until it touches the tidal curve.

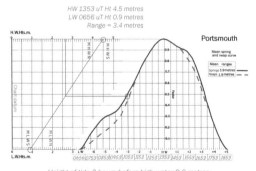

Height of tide 3 hours before high water 2.6 metres

Using the tidal curve

- From this point draw a horizontal line until it reaches the line joining today's HW and LW heights.

- From this point draw a vertical line to the height of tide scales at the top or bottom of the chart.

- This is the height of tide at the required time.
- The process can be reversed to find the time that the tide will be at a particular height – useful for crossing shallow water.

Another Way of Looking at the Process

- It's not always obvious why the height of tide part of the calculation works as it does.
- If we turn the tidal curve on its side, the method becomes much more obvious.
- The chart datum is coloured red on the bottom of the chart.
- The height of today's HW is on the left and the height of LW is on the right.
- The line joining the two heights represents how the height of tide varies from HW to LW.
- Where the 'time line' hits the 'tidal height line' we can read off the height of tide.

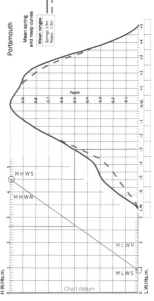

Or look at it this way!

Secondary Ports

Data are published for secondary ports to allow calculation of times and heights of HW and LW. There are complicated ways for obtaining differences at times other than those shown in the differences tables. However, I believe that for most purposes, the information may be obtained by 'inspection'.

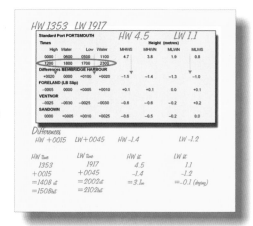

Tidal differences at Bembridge

- Draw an arrow between the HW times shown at approximately the correct proportion of the distance between them – for instance, if the time of HW at the standard port were 0400, the arrow would be two-thirds the distance between 0000 and 0600, that is closer to 0600 than 0000. At this stage, we must work in the same time zone as the tide table. In this case we have not yet *added* the one hour for BST.

158

- Note, a time difference of 0020 means 00 hours and 20 minutes, a time difference of 0115 means 01 hours and 15 minutes. There's no full stop or colon between them. 0115 does not mean 115 minutes!

- Use the same procedure for the time of LW.

- Similarly, draw arrows for the heights of HW and LW, according to their closeness to springs or neaps.

- This allows us to read off the values of the differences directly from the table.

- Apply these differences to the times and heights of HW and LW for the standard port to get the data for our secondary port

- We can now adjust for local time, that is add 1 hour for BST in this case.

SHOM Tidal Predictions

The equivalent to the UKHO in France is SHOM. SHOM offers several methods of calculating the height of tide at any particular time. The simplest is the 'rule of twelfths', which is often sufficient for curves close to being in the shape of a sine wave. Also offered is a mathematical solution able to account for any skew in the sine wave.

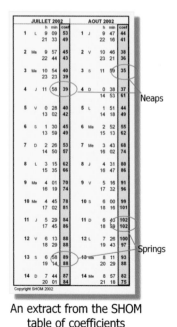

An extract from the SHOM table of coefficients

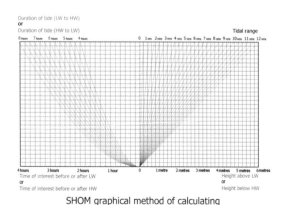

SHOM graphical method of calculating height of tide

The easiest method for boat owners is their graphical solution.

Tidal Height Coefficients

SHOM provides an annual table of tidal coefficients to distinguish how high and how low are the heights of tide relative to mean sea level (niveau moyen), which has a coefficient of 0 (zero). Spring tides have a coefficient of approximately 1.0, whilst neap tides have a coefficient of approximately 0.5. HAT and LAT are equivalent to 1.2 and zero, respectively. The diagram shows the SHOM definitions and their approximate UKHO equivalents.

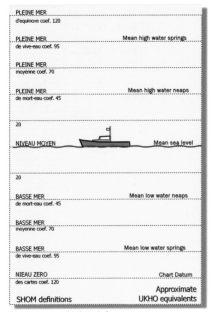

SHOM Graphical Method

The graphical method can be found in 'votre livre de board', published annually by Bloc Marine(www.blocmarine.com).

The graph used for the solution is shown here and here's how to use it to calculate the height of tide on 14th July at 15:06 French Summer Time:

SHOM definitions

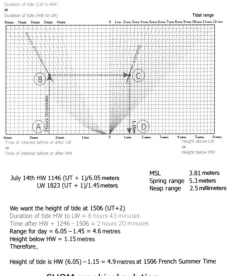

July 14th HW 1146 (UT + 1)/6.05 meters
LW 1823 (UT + 1)/1.45 meters

MSL   3.81 meters
Spring range 5.3 meters
Neap range   2.5 millimeters

We want the height of tide at 1506 (UT+2)
Duration of tide HW to LW = 6 hours 43 minutes
Time after HW + 1246 − 1506 = 2 hours 20 minutes
Range for day = 6.05 − 1.45 = 4.6 metres
Height below HW = 1.15 metres
Therefore,

Height of tide is HW (6.05) − 1.15 = 4.9 metres at 1506 French Summer Time

SHOM graphical sulution

- Note the times and heights of HW and LW for Cherbourg.
- Calculate the time after HW that you want to know the height of tide (this can also be done relative to LW) (2 hour 20 minutes – Point A).

- Calculate the duration from HW to LW (6 hour 43 minutes – Point B).
- Calculate the range of the tide – HW ht minus LW ht (4.6 m – Point C).
- Point D shows the height of tide at 15:06 *below* the height of HW.
- If you use the time interval *before* LW, the answer will be the height of tide *above* LW.

Differences at Secondary Port

The method is almost identical to that used by UKHO. Remember to correct for local time *after* you've done all the other calculations.

NOM DU PORT	Niveau moyen m	HEURES AU PORT PRINCIPAL DE REFERENCE				HAUTEURS AU PORT PRINCIPAL DE REFERENCE			
		Pleines mers		Basses mers		Pleines mers		Basses mers	
		VE h min	ME h min	VE h min	ME h min	VE m	ME m	VE m	ME m
CHERBOURG	3,81	9 45 21 45	3 30 15 30	10 00 22 00	4 20 16 20	6,4	5,05	2,5	1,1
		Correction aux heures				correction aux hauteurs			
Saint-Vasst-la-Hougue	4,12	+0 50	+1 20	+1 15	+1 20	+0.35	+0.45	0.0	-0.05
VE is equivalent to spring tides; ME is equivalent to neap tides									

SHOM differences from standard ports

Tidal Streams

When planning a passage, plotting an estimated position, or calculating a course to steer (CTS), we will need to know the direction and speed of any tidal stream. This information is provided in 'tidal atlases', which can be bought as a separate publication, found in almanacs or on some charts.

- Each diagram of the atlas shows the average direction and speed over a period of 1 hour.
- Each diagram is for a specific '1 hour' relative to the time of high water at a reference port.
- The reference port may be for a port some distance from the area covered by the atlas.
- Do not assume that the reference port is the same port that you will use for your tidal height calculations.
- The atlas will make it clear which port is to be used.

A Tidal Atlas

Shown here is a tidal atlas for an area to the east of the Isle of Wight. The diagrams are labelled from HW −6 (hours) to HW +6 (hours). Each diagram is valid from half an hour before the stated time until half an hour after the stated time and is the averages for the whole hour. There are two values for the speed, the higher being for spring tides and the lower for neap tides. It's quite valid for the practical navigator to estimate the values in between.

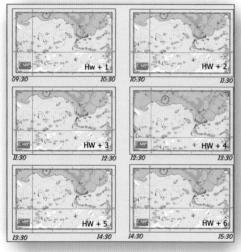

Tidal atlas – page 2

HW is at 08:00 UTC - 09:00 BST

Label the bottom corners of each chartlet with the start and finish times for that tidal diagram, that is half an hour before until half an hour after the 'central' time of that particular tidal 'time'. This shows the time that each diagram applies to. This makes life much easier when you use the tidal atlas.

Tidal atlas – page 1

- Label the HW diagram with the time of HW.

- Label the left hand bottom corner with half an hour before HW and the right hand bottom corner with half an hour after HW.

- This gives the times between which this diagram can be used.

- All the other diagrams need to be labelled only with their 'start and finish' times.

- The diagram for HW −3 is shown.

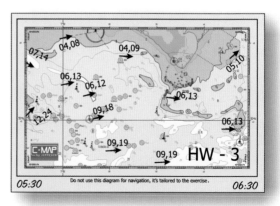

The tidal atlas diagram from 05:30 until 06:30

Tidal Diamonds

Many charts have 'tidal diamonds' marked on them and a table showing the value of the direction and speeds of the tides at these discrete points. They are fine for estimating the tide at a particular point for such operations as diving and fishing, but are cumbersome to use for planning and plotting purposes.

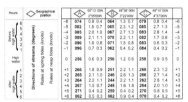

Tidal stream data for each hour before and after the time of high water

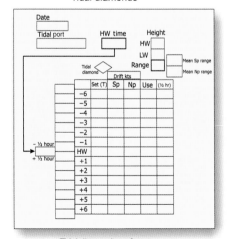

The lettered diamonds indicate the position for each set of tidal stream data

Based on high Water Dover

The table of tidal stream data

Tidal diamonds

Just as when using a tidal atlas, each tabulated value for a diamond is the average for the 1-hour period. However, there's insufficient room on the tables to label the values with a time. I've found that many people make mistakes when working out which 'hour' to use, so you may find it helpful to use a pro forma to do this. You can print off a proforma from Wiley Nautical's website www.wileynautical.co.uk.

You don't need to fill in all the blanks, just those that you need, as shown. As before, the actual speeds, if not neaps or springs can be estimated.

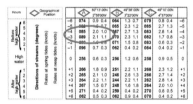

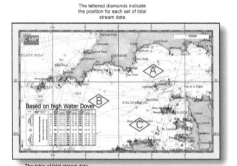

Tidal diamond pro-forma

Tidal diamond calculations

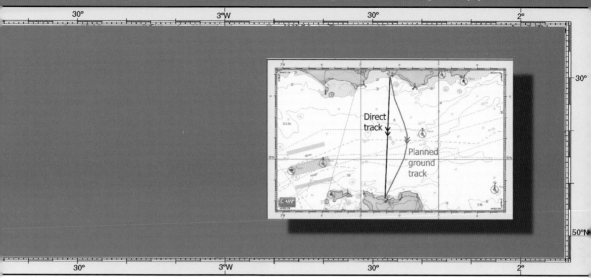

Tidal Planning and Plotting

A Long Passage Using a Single CTS

Where will the Tide Take You?

An open water passage will require the use of a number of tidal diagrams. You could, of course, calculate a new course to steer every hour, but if the passage is to be 'across tide' this is a very inefficient way to work. You will always be pointing into tide and a 12 hour passage could easily take an hour or more to complete using this strategy.

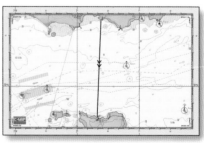

Passage chart

A Long Passage Using a Single CTS

On a long passage leg, a single course to steer can be calculated using many tidal vectors all in one operation and this is much more efficient.

- Draw ground track to destination.
- Measure ground distance.
- Estimate passage time.
- Label tidal stream atlas with times from the tide table.

- Draw ground track on tidal atlas diagram.
- Mark a strip of paper with hourly progress marks and label the ETA at each point.

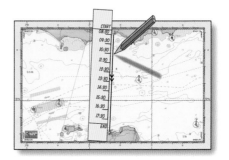

- Moving from one tidal atlas diagram to the next, estimate the tidal current at each point.

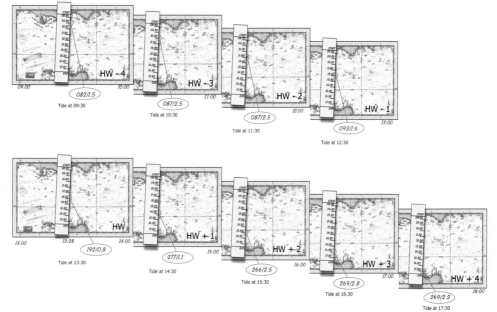

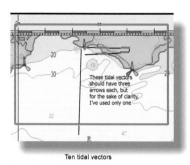

Ten tidal vectors

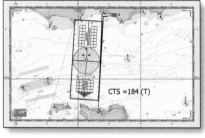

CTS =184 (T)

Course to steer

- Mark in the tidal vectors at the start point on the passage chart.
- Measure the estimated passage time from the last tidal vector to where it cuts the ground track.

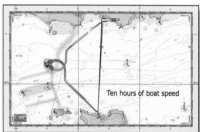

Ten hours of boat speed

Mark off water distance covered in ten hours

- This is the single course to steer.

Where will the Tide Take You?

It seems common sense to enquire where the boat will travel on its way to its destination. Indeed, how can you monitor the boat's progress if you don't know where it's supposed to be?

This is easily accomplished by plotting *estimated positions* along the way before you even start. This has the added advantage that should you have to resort to plotting EPs, it's already been done at your leisure. So how do you accomplish that?

- Draw your direct track on your passage chart.
- Mark hourly progress points on the chart.

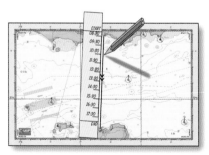

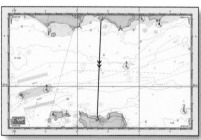

Passage chart

- Draw lines perpendicular to the direct track long enough to accommodate the maximum tidal effect.
- Draw a track grid parallel to

direct track with lines at 1 nautical mile spacing. Theoretically, this grid should be parallel to the

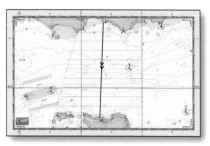

Draw lines for the expected progress each hour

CTS, but in reality it's easier to use the direct track, which also makes the grid useful for plotting GPS positions on passage.

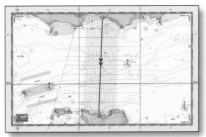

Draw parallel 'cross-track error' lines

- Make a table of running tidal offsets for each hour.

Direction	Speed	Offset
076	1.0	1.0
082	1.5	2.5
087	2.5	5.0
087	2.5	7.5
093	1.6	9.1
192	0.8	9.1
277	1.1	8.0
266	2.5	5.5
269	2.8	2.7
269	2.2	0.5

Tidal offsets

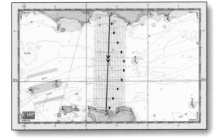

Mark in tidal offsets along route

- Mark the offsets on the grid.

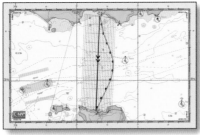

Draw ground track though tidal offsets

- Joint the offsets with a continuous line.
- This line is the planned ground track.

Planned ground track using single CTS

- When you steer the single CTS, you should follow this planned ground track. Any error is the error compared with the planned ground track, not compared with the direct track.
- If you are monitoring GPS cross-track error, the error should mirror the running tidal offsets, not remain at zero.

Credits

It would not have been possible to illustrate this book in the way that I had envisaged without the charts and simulations made possible by the cooperation of C-Map, Euronav, Lightmaster Software and Standard Horizon.

Charts Have Been Drawn Using Software Supplied by

C-Map with the kind cooperation of Mr Paul Sumpner, MD of C-Map, UK.
  Euronav (seaPro) with the kind cooperation of Dr Brian Morris, MD.

Radar Simulations

Lightmaster Software with the kind cooperation of Mr Martin Quaintance FRIN.

Chartplotter Simulations

C-Map with the kind cooperation of Mr Paul Sumpner, MD of C-Map, UK.
  Standard Horizon with the kind cooperation of Yeasu, UK.

'Space' Pictures

Some of the diagrams use images of the earth courtesy of NASA and this imagery may be viewed online at Visible Earth. (http://visibleearth.nasa.gov/)

World Currents Chart

US Naval Laboratory

Ocean currents – *This image is a copy of **ocean_currents_1943.jpg**, a map from the map collection of the* Perry-Castañeda Library (PCL) of the University of Texas at Austin. *According to the FAQs it is in the **public domain**.*

Tidal Height and Tidal Currents

Diagrams and data for UK – UKHO and Nautical Data Ltd.
Diagrams and data for France – SHOM and Bloc Marine.
Diagrams and data for USA – NOAA.

Standard Port PORTSMOUTH							
Times					**Height (metres)**		
High	Water	Low	Water	MHWS	MHWN	MLWN	MLWS
0000	0600	0500	1100	4.7	3.8	1.9	0.8
1200	1800	1700	2300				
Differences BEMBRIDGE HARBOUR							
+0020	0000	+0100	+0020	-1.5	-1.4	-1.3	-1.0
FORELAND (LB Slip)							
-0005	0000	+0005	+0010	+0.1	+0.1	0.0	+0.1
VENTNOR							
-0025	-0030	-0025	-0030	-0.8	-0.6	-0.2	+0.2
SANDOWN							
0000	+0005	+0010	+0025	-0.6	-0.5	-0.2	0.0

Tidal differences at Bembridge

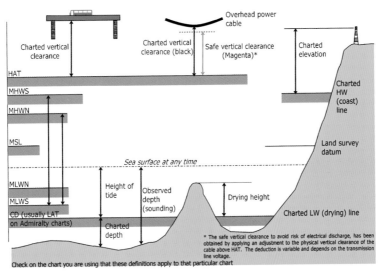

Tide levels and height references

Tides are UT + 1
(French standard time)

JUILLET 2002	Heures		Haut
	h	min	m
13 S	5	21	**1,05**
	11	00	**6,1**
	17	37	**1,3**
	23	11	**6,3**
14 D	6	06	**1,05**
	11	46	**6,05**
	18	23	**1,45**
	23	58	**6,2**
15 L	6	53	**1,15**
	12	33	**5,9**
	19	12	**1,6**

For French Summer Time
add 1 hour

Extract from Cherbourg
tide tables

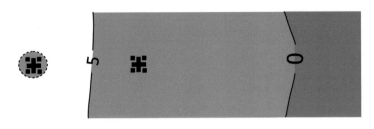

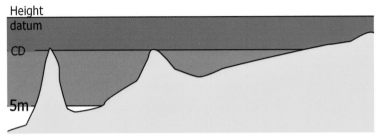

Rock awash at the level of Chart Datum

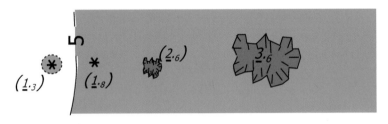

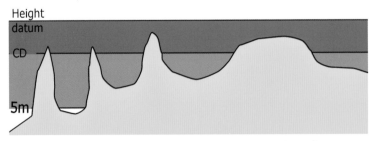

Rock which covers and uncovers, height
above Chart Datum, where known

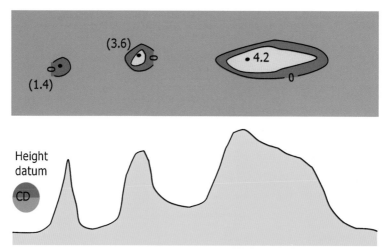

Rock which does not cover,
height above chart datum

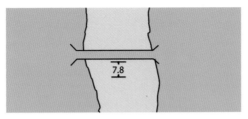

Clearance under a bridge

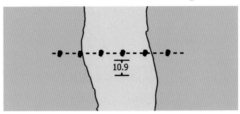

Clearance under a cable

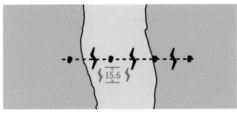

Safe clearance under a power
transmission cable where
published otherwise the actual
clearance is shown in black

Vertical clearances

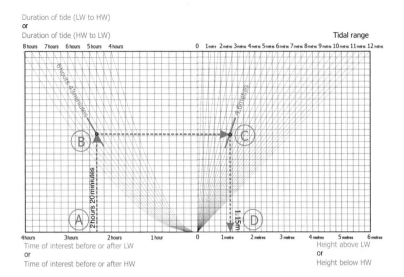

Duration of tide (LW to HW)
or
Duration of tide (HW to LW)

Tidal range

July 14th HW 1146 (UT + 1)/6.05 meters
LW 1823 (UT + 1)/1.45 meters

MSL   3.81 meters
Spring range   5.3 meters
Neap range   2.5 millimeters

We want the height of tide at 1506 (UT+2)
Duration of tide HW to LW = 6 hours 43 minutes
Time after HW + 1246 − 1506 = 2 hours 20 minutes
Range for day = 6.05 − 1.45 = 4.6 metres
Height below HW = 1.15 metres
Therefore,

Height of tide is HW (6.05) − 1.15 = 4.9 metres at 1506 French Summer Time

SHOM graphical sulution

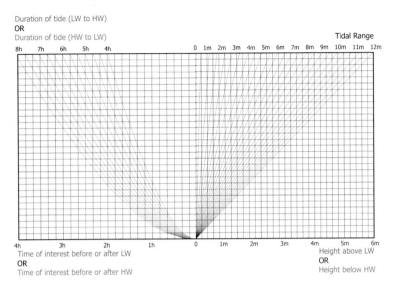

Duration of tide (LW to HW)
OR
Duration of tide (HW to LW)

Tidal Range

8h 7h 6h 5h 4h   0 1m 2m 3m 4m 5m 6m 7m 8m 9m 10m 11m 12m

4h   3h   2h   1h   0   1m   2m   3m   4m   5m   6m
Time of interest before or after LW   Height above LW
OR   OR
Time of interest before or after HW   Height below HW

SHOM graphical method of calculating
height of tide

NOM DU PORT	Niveau moyen m	HEURES AU PORT PRINCIPAL DE REFERENCE				HAUTEURS AU PORT PRINCIPAL DE REFERENCE			
		Pleines mers		Basses mers		Pleines mers		Basses mers	
		VE h min	ME h min	VE h min	ME h min	VE m	ME m	VE m	ME m
CHERBOURG	3,81	9 45 21 45	3 30 15 30	10 00 22 00	4 20 16 20	6,4	5,05	2,5	1,1
		Correction aux heures				correction aux hauteurs			
Saint-Vasst-la-Hougue	4,12	+0 50	+1 20	+1 15	+1 20	+0,35	+0,45	0,0	-0,05
VE is equivalent to Spring tides; ME is equivalent to Neap tides									

SHOM differences from standard ports

JUILLET 2002				AOUT 2002			
		h	min	coef		h	min	coef
1	L	9	09	53	1	J	9	47	44
		21	33	49			22	16	41
2	Ma	9	57	45	2	V	10	46	38
		22	44	43			23	21	36
3	Me	10	54	40	3	S	11	59	35
		23	23	39					
4	J	11	58	39	4	D	0	38	37
							14	53	61
5	V	0	28	40	5	L	1	51	44
		13	02	42			14	18	49
6	S	1	30	45	6	Ma	2	52	55
		13	59	49			15	13	62
7	D	2	26	53	7	Me	3	43	68
		14	50	57			16	02	74
8	L	3	15	62	8	J	4	31	80
		15	35	66			16	47	86
9	Ma	4	01	70	9	V	5	16	91
		16	19	74			17	32	96
10	Me	4	45	78	10	S	6	00	99
		17	02	81			18	16	101
11	J	5	29	84	11	D	6	43	102
		17	45	86			18	59	102
12	V	6	13	88	12	L	7	26	100
		18	29	88			19	43	97
13	S	6	58	89	13	Ma	8	11	93
		19	14	88			20	29	88
14	D	7	44	87	14	Me	8	57	82
		20	01	84			21	18	75

Copyright SHOM 2002

Neaps

Springs

An extract from the SHOM
table of coefficients

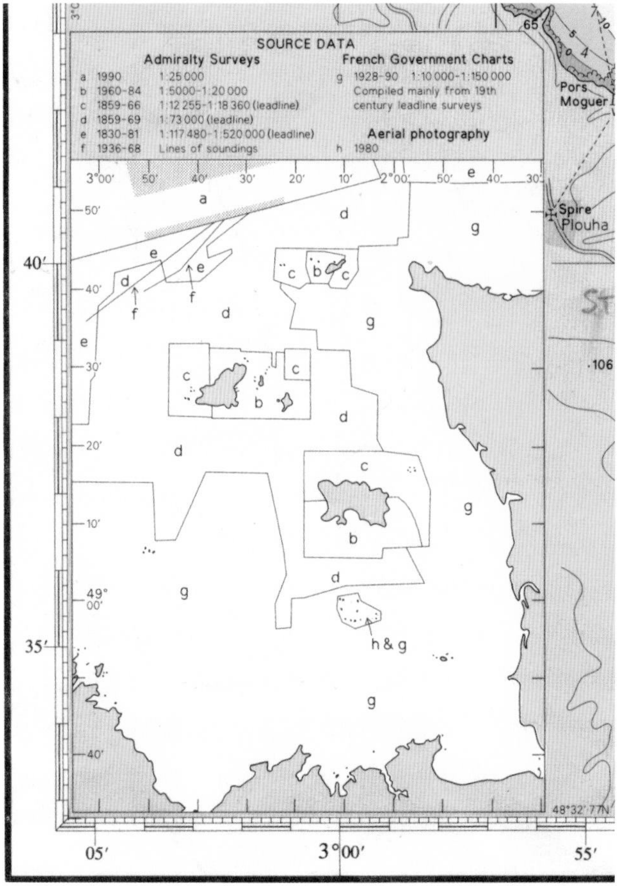
SOURCE DATA
Admiralty Surveys
a 1990 1:25 000
b 1960-84 1:5000-1:20 000
c 1859-66 1:12 255-1:18 360 (leadline)
d 1859-69 1:73 000 (leadline)
e 1830-81 1:117 480-1:520 000 (leadline)
f 1936-68 Lines of soundings
French Government Charts
g 1928-90 1:10 000-1:150 000
Compiled mainly from 19th
century leadline surveys
Aerial photography
h 1980
Pors Moguer
Spire Plouha
h & g
48°32'.77N
05'
3°00'
55'

UK Hydrographic Office source diagram

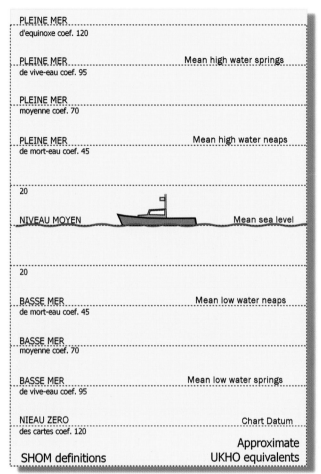

SHOM definitions

TIME ZONE (UT)

For summer Time add ONE Hour in **non-shaded areas**

ENGLAND - PORTSMOUTH
Times and heights of high and low waters

JUNE   JULY

	Time	m		Time	m		Time	m		Time	m
16 SA ○	0510 1202 1729	0.8 4.7 0.9	**1** SU	0456 1147 1714 2355	1.1 4.4 1.2 4.4	**16** M	0005 0546 1241 1802	4.6 0.8 4.6 1.0	**1** W	0019 0601 1254 1820	4.6 0.7 4.7 0.8
17 SU	0016 0557 1252 1815	4.7 0.8 4.7 1.0	**2** M	0535 1228 1154	1.0 4.5 1.1	**17** TU	0048 0626 1322 1843	4.5 0.8 4.6 1.0	**2** TH	0101 0641 1335 1901	4.6 0.6 4.7 0.8
18 M	0102 0642 1339 1900	4.6 0.8 4.6 1.1	**3** TU	0034 0615 1310 1835	4.5 0.9 4.5 1.1	**18** W	0127 0704 1401 1920	4.4 0.9 4.5 1.1	**3** F	0143 0722 1416 1943	4.6 0.6 4.7 0.8
19 TU	0147 0725 1426 1945	4.4 1.0 4.5 1.3	**4** W	0115 0656 1353 1917	4.4 0.9 4.5 1.1	**19** TH	0204 0739 1437 1956	4.3 1.0 4.5 1.2	**4** SA	0226 0803 1458 2027	4.5 0.8 4.6 1.0
20 W	0231 0807 1511 2029	4.3 1.1 4.4 1.4	**5** TH	0158 0739 1437 2002	4.4 0.9 4.5 1.1	**20** F	0240 0812 1511 0232	4.2 1.2 4.3 1.4	**5** SU ☽	0311 0848 1543 2116	4.4 1.0 4.5 1.2

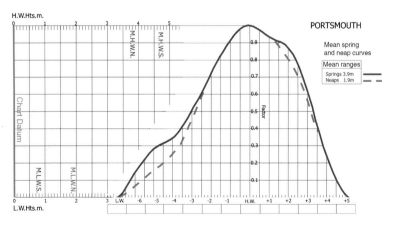

H.W.Hts.m.

PORTSMOUTH

Mean spring and neap curves

Mean ranges	
Springs 3.9m	
Neaps 1.9m	

Chart Datum

M.H.W.N. M.H.W.S.

M.L.W.S. M.L.W.N.

Factor

L.W.Hts.m.

Tidal curve for Portsmouth

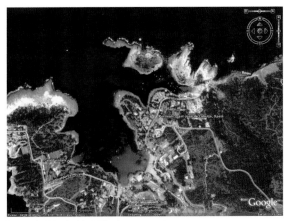

Sourced: Google Maps™ mapping service

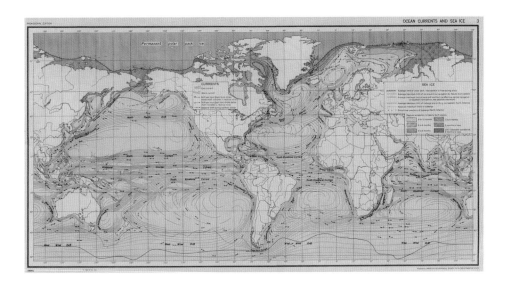

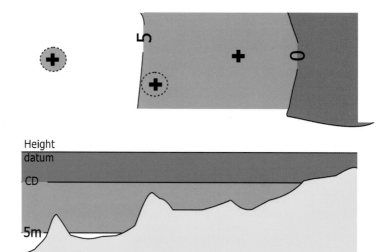

Underwater rock over which the depth
is unknown, but which is considered
dangerous to surface navigation

Lifeboats

'Flat calm or force 10. I always wear one.'

Whether they're training or out on a shout, RNLI crew members always wear lifejackets. It's a rule informed by years of experience. They know that, whatever the weather, the sea's extremely unpredictable – and can turn at a moment's notice. They see people caught out all the time. People who've risked, or even lost their lives as a result. The fact is, a lifejacket will buy you vital time in the water – and could even save your life. But only if you're wearing it.

For advice on choosing a lifejacket and how to wear it correctly, call us on 0800 328 0600 (UK) or 1800 789 589 (RoI) or visit our website rnli.org.uk/seasafety/lifejackets

Useless unless worn